Your World is Exploding

How Social Media is Changing
Everything—and how you need to
Change with it.

Christopher G. Dessi

To my parents Patricia and Adrian — with love,
admiration and gratitude.

TABLE OF CONTENTS

ACKNOWLEDGMENTS

To my beautiful wife Laura for being there every step of this journey and for supporting everything that I do. Thank you for whispering in my ear in my darkest moments to assure me I can do anything I set my mind to. I love you. To my gorgeous daughters Talia and Olivia for showing me the true meaning of life. To my brother Mark, his wife, Antonella and their amazing children Sophia, Julia and Luke for their love, and support. To Papa for watching over me. To Mike Pace, Steve Singlak, and David Hufnagel for their unconditional friendship. To my in-laws Anthony and Maryanne Guiglotto for their love and support.

To Gary Vaynerchuk for igniting my burning passion for social media. To Jeff Pearlman, whose time, effort and insight were invaluable throughout the process of writing this book — and for naming the book too!

To everyone seeking a new journey in life, this book is dedicated to you. I hope it helps to guide you to true fulfillment.

PROLOGUE

It was 2007, and I worked at Azoogle (now, Epic Media Group) a multi-million dollar ad-network. We ruled the tooth whitening, colon cleansing, date getting, and ring tone peddling portion of the Internet. The founders, Joe Speiser, and Alex Zhardanovsky had created one of the most amazing work environments I'd ever experienced. We all worked like crazy, churned out sales, and made good money. I loved every minute of it. Well, almost every minute. It all changed when I was given my seat in our new office.

The office was almost fully open plan, and I had the worst seat in the house. Our previous office was gorgeous, but too small for our growing company. In this office, we had to endure the constant din of power tools throughout most of the day. Dust, noise, and faulty air conditioning aren't a good start to any working day, but we understood we had moved to this new larger space because we were growing and improving.

To get to my desk after stepping off the elevator, you had to navigate over the "red carpet" of dirty cardboard protecting the floor, which had been strategically placed by construction workers. The builders worked around the clock to eventually transform our dustbin into a stunning work place (I didn't stay long enough to experience the finished product). As visitors entered the main office space my desk was the first thing they'd see. Or more accurately— the growing bald spot on the back of my head was the first thing they'd see. Engrossed in my work, I usually didn't even notice the arrival of a new visitor. Delivery people would drop their packages with me. Interviewees would nervously ask to see the boss. Personally, I felt ready for the next step in my career, and my new seating arrangement was the nudge I needed to make a change. I also desperately wanted to be a vice president. While I loved my colleagues, and Joe & Alex had given me the opportunity to flourish, I was ready to leave. I respected my boss Brett Lofgren, but I wanted his job, and he wasn't planning on going anywhere.

At that moment, in the middle of the open floor plan in 2007, I decided I wanted out. I wanted more control, and the freedom to do things my way. So I decided to take control of my destiny. And I started a blog.

Your World is Exploding

Christopher G. Dessi

1 AWAKENING

"There are no random acts...We are all connected...You can no more separate one life from another than you can separate a breeze from the wind..."

— *Mitch Albom*

Fox Studios, New York City

As I stepped into the studio I felt the breeze from the air conditioning wash over me. This made me happy because I tend to run hot. You can usually gauge my level of anxiety by the number of sweat beads layered atop my upper lip. My current situation should have seen my anxiety level shooting through the roof, but I felt surprisingly calm. That I was about to face the greatest opportunity of my career wasn't lost on me, but I was prepared. I felt good, calm even. I was told to sit at a large desk on a riser. The producer spoke to me, but nothing really registered. I was absorbed by my surroundings. It felt as if I were sitting at the control center, piloting my body through this surreal experience. She hooked a monitor to my belt, then ran a wire under my blazer, and asked me in which ear I'd like the bud placed? "I guess my right one," I said. I could feel the lights on my face. Not good. Warmth is my enemy. Now I could feel the sweat on my back, and I knew my face would erupt any minute. However, there was nothing I could do. I really didn't want to mess up the makeup. I certainly hadn't expected to have that thought when I woke up this morning.

"Chris, can you hear this OK?" I was staring directly into the camera when I heard a voice in my ear. This threw me off track. I'd been thinking about what I wanted to say in my head, and the voice knocked me off kilter. As the voice registered in my brain, I noticed the camera moving closer. I was a little confused to see that the cameras were remote control, but that wasn't what kept me preoccupied. "Yes," I said. "I've got it."

"OK folks, here we go," said the director. I heard the intro music playing and I watched the show's graphics fly across the screen in front of me.

Ernie Anastos, the Emmy Award winning news anchor whom I'd met two minutes beforehand started to speak. His voice was strong, assertive, and confident. "Fired over Facebook posts, a first of its kind case..." he boomed, I heard Ernie talking, and I saw him on the screen in front of me. He was only about 50 feet away, but we would be talking to each other on a split screen and I was told to look directly into the camera. I had trouble following this minor direction because this is also where the teleprompter was located, so I began to read what Ernie was saying. Then suddenly I started to panic. Cool Chris had left the building! My heart beating so hard I could literally hear the blood swooshing in my ears.

"STOP," yelled the producer. "What happened?"

"Tech problem with the intro graphics, let's start again from the top." Ernie turned to me.

"So Chris, when is your baby daughter due again?" I started to answer when the producer declared..."OK, here we go folks, from the top."

Intro music..."Breathe this time," I thought. "And stop reading the teleprompter you meat-head." That gave me the five seconds I needed to get myself together. Is this really happening? Will I really be on television, or will this end up on the cutting room floor? Oh man, here it comes, breathe, smile, and focus.

"Joining us right now is Chris Dessi, an executive at Drive Action Digital. First off Chris, this is groundbreaking, a first of its kind case... what's your reaction to this story tonight?"

"Well, my training isn't legal; however you're correct, the implications of this case are tremendous..." and so it continued. Somehow, in an inexplicable twist of fate, I was now a social media expert commentator on Fox television.

I decided to write this book on a chilly March evening in Poughkeepsie, NY. I'd just spent the better part of three hours interacting with and lecturing to students at Marist College. The topic I covered had a risqué title "How the F*ck Can Social media Get Me a Job," and was filled with silliness and humor, but there was nothing silly about the message: if students start leveraging social media immediately they'll effectively turn the tables on the manner in which they gain employment. I was taken aback by the overwhelmingly positive reception I received. The students were ready to hear my message. They knew things had changed, but they didn't know where to start. So on the drive home from Marist, while still glowing from the energy those students had given me, I turned to my wife Laura, and said, "I have to write a book."

We are all connected

The astronomical explosion of social media in recent years is a spiritual awakening, not a technological one. I'll give you a minute to let that sink in. I'll also apologize if you bought this book hoping to get a textbook guide to social media success. I was going to write that book, but I think this book is more important. This book transcends technology. Plus, there are enough great books about the tactical aspect of social media, itemizing steps to meet your goals, (business or personal). These are all great books, but, none of the guidance they offer (while reputable) will work for you unless you understand why social media is so powerful. Stay with me.

Social media has nothing to do with a specific company or technology. Social media will not die if Facebook dissolves tomorrow. Do you remember how popular Friendster and MySpace used to be? There will continue to be social media even if Twitter sends its last Tweet. This is because human beings make social media powerful. Social media is an extension of our collective unconscious. Social media is our digital spirit. Don't fret – I'll offer tactical instruction here, however I'll also share with you the energy behind the tactics, and why I think that essence is the key to succeeding in social media.

Wash it all away, take away the platforms, the dashboards, the branded color schemes, the technology and what do you have? You have humanity. Take away the strategy, the tenants of marketing, the etiquette of social media, the unwritten rules for "engagement," and what do you have? Again, the common denominator is humanity.

At our core we all know this is true. We know that when our friends write a status update on Facebook that is pure, from the heart and spontaneous, it has the power to make our hearts pound and our faces blush. We also know that when there is a lack of truth in this environment we can feel it just as if we were sitting across the room from that person. We feel the status update. We are tickled by truths that are shared. We become emotional at proclamations of truth. We latch onto those who we see as leaders. Those who are tapped into this collective unconscious and who function at a higher level have trouble replicating their successes for others because they do it naturally. It's like asking a professional football player

"How many strides, cut backs, and leaps will it take for me to score a touchdown just like you?" It doesn't work that way. You need to understand the goal, trust your ability, and then the "how" will unfold right in front of you.

The best way to approach social media is to understand that there are tactics you need to follow. However, in order to make what you're creating a success you need to fully comprehend the essence of what social media can be. Social media in and of itself is by no means spiritual. However all media, when done properly, is somewhat of a spiritual dance. The best commercials move us. Good or bad - fear or laughter, or tears. The best books do the same, television shows, movies, etcetera. Media, this animal on its own is "US." It's our collective unconscious. It's our spirit.

How many times have you seen people moved to tears while listening to music? What is that? It's simple. It's the truth that we're all connected. We can feel each other when we're all firing on the same frequency. Those who can tap into this river of human energy are those who are the most successful in life. Those who can tap into these rapids are also those who understand the way social media works the best. They conduct themselves appropriately because they don't know any different.

Now that you know the truth about social media, I need you to trust me. Social media works I promise. For you to get the most from this book, you need to let go. Let go of your preconceived notions of social media. Get Facebook's iconic blue and white logo out of your mind. Erase the Twitter bird, and fail whale. Open yourself to humanity. Open yourself to the collective unconscious of social media. Open your heart, and enjoy this ride. I hope it rings true for you.

The Secret to Social Media

The social media secret is a big one! You have access to free tools to amplify your connection with other human beings. Instead of a solo thought, you have the ability to share that thought, and spread the energy behind that thought. When you complain via social media, you receive more complainers. When you offer praise via social media, you receive praise. I actively try to "right" my thoughts in my own internal spiritual life. I meditate, quiet my mind, and share. The moments when I'm most authentic I am most often re-Tweeted, shared and commented on. The moments when I'm false, and lose sight of my true intent, I fall upon deaf ears.

Your World is Exploding

After the traumatic events of September 11, 2001, I found myself seeking spiritual support and guidance. For the first time in my life I felt as if I'd awakened from a lifelong slumber. I had gone through the motions of life, but I couldn't say that I'd ever truly lived. I was playing it safe, happy to dedicate my intellectual power to my social life. My weekends consisted of night clubbing, recreational drug use, and serial womanizing. My workweeks were there to help me recover from the previous weekend's debauchery. I did the bare minimum to survive. I'd make a few sales calls here and there, but I was spending more time on dating sites, than on sales proposals. I was making just enough money to squeak by. I wasn't fulfilling my full potential. I was certainly misguided. September 11, while horrible, helped me discover myself, and take my first step on my journey to self–discovery. The first step (for me) was yoga. After living through the horrors of September 11, I needed an outlet. I decided to ignore my self-conscious inclinations, and took my first yoga class. I was the only guy in the class. I felt awkward, silly and clumsy in those early days. But I was starting to scratch the surface of a larger reality. I was discovering a power within that I'd only before read about. I could now do things with my body that I previously didn't think possible. I began falling into deep meditative states that allowed me to see my world with a clarity I'd never even dreamt about. I was experiencing an awakening. This awakening attracted amazing business success, although I had made a mistake. I didn't focus on true fulfillment in success. I only focused on monetary success. In the years following September 11, I'd been named vice president of a multi-national advertising network: I'd bought a home in bucolic Chappaqua, NY and had just furnished the entire home in one preposterous shopping spree. I should have been on top of the world. I should have felt fulfilled. I didn't, because my intent for business success was misguided. I saw financial success, but felt malcontented.

My goal for you is to discover true fulfillment via social media. I'm going to show you how.

Truth

After I started my blog in 2007, I stuck to generating content about business. I would select an article in a trade publication and offer my opinion about the piece. I would get some readers, and I felt good about the work I was generating. I moved into my vice president role, and continued to offer my business insight on my blog. Then I was let go. I had a decision to make. Would I pretend that I left this dream job on my own, or would I honestly blog about my experience? We all tell ourselves lies. We create excuses, put up walls, and point fingers. It's not easy to find your truth. The first step for true success is to stop telling lies, and take inventory. Forgive those you hold grudges against. Free yourself from the expectations of others. Put your health first, and ask yourself what will truly make me experience fulfillment? I decided I would allow my readers to learn that I was let go, and I blogged about the experience. I spoke about my depression, my drinking and my coping with being out of work. I gained a whole new readership, and I purged my demons. Once you've answered the question "what will truly make me experience fulfillment," then you can begin your journey to discover the true spirituality of social media. If you decide to start a blog and base the content on what you're currently doing at work, and that work is not fulfilling, you won't succeed. The moment you begin to generate content from your heart, it'll pour out. You'll never experience writer's block. You'll wake up in the middle of the night with ideas to blog about. You'll feel a light flicker inside you that you know you must share with those in your social network. You'll crave to have a larger audience with which to share your message. See if you can recall the last time you were working on something and it felt as if time had dissolved. Moments became hours, and hours became days. You didn't seek motivation from outside sources; you just followed your intuition. This is your goal in social media. I don't want you to lament over every wall post, Tweet, blog post, or video blog. If you're generating content from the right place, you'll experience success. If your heart is in it, and you feel content in your bones you'll succeed.

Fear

Wael Ghonim was born Dec 23, 1980 in Cairo, Egypt. In 2011, Ghonim, (a Google employee) found himself gravely concerned about the suspicious circumstances in which his fellow Egyptian citizen Khaled Mohamed died. He believed he'd witnessed his government do something abominable. Outraged, he launched a Facebook page in protest, thus igniting a revolution. Ghonim didn't fire a gun, throw a Molotov cocktail, or induce a riot. He simply started a Facebook page called "We are all Khaled Saeed." This singular act, via social media, helped to trigger what is now being referred to as the Arab Spring. All protests in 2011 have one common denominator: social media.

Your World is Exploding

I'm not asking you to start a revolution, I'm asking you to be fearless. As I'm writing these words, they'll fall on some deaf ears. However, for others — these words will feel like a kick to the belly. They'll wake you up from your own personal slumber.

Your own path will be different than mine. You'll define yourself and gain fulfillment via your own journey. But it will never happen if you're fearful. You can't create if you're fearful of others opinions, or fearful of repercussions from your work in social media. Allow yourself to be free. Engaging in social media can be scary at first. It may take you weeks to figure out what to blog about. Start small. If you can't think of anything, get smaller. If you're a cook, don't blog about food, don't even blog about ingredients. Start with the tools. Start with your favorite knife. Start with how the knife feels in your hand. Start with the perfect balance of the tool; describe how your knife is an extension of yourself and how you cannot imagine creating a dish without this secret weapon. Start small, and the rest will come.

What do you have to lose? I mean, really lose? If the answer is that you may look foolish, then I challenge you. Actually, better yet — I beg you to let go of your fear. Don't fear the detractors. Instead focus on the good that you'll do by leveraging social media. Visualize your next blog post reaching someone who is moved to tears by your content. Feel that you've just inspired someone. Own the idea that you have knowledge about something that someone will love to hear. It may be how to make something, it may be your opinion about someone, it may be that you love the outdoors, and you want to share that passion. Visualize that connection. Embrace your tribe. Realize that you can reach them via technology. You can blog about something that will strongly and positively change someone's life. You can connect with someone who is just as oppressed as you. You can shine a light on darkness that must be exposed. You can create. You can start a revolution. You must be fearless.

You may be wondering — "who am I?" Well, who are you to *not* share yourself with the world? We are all connected, and we all deserve to be heard. We all have something to offer. We all have passion. We all have something to say. We all have an opinion. We all have love. Own that power. Own your passion and share it. Don't be afraid of your own light. There is no reason why you shouldn't share your passion with the world. In fact, it's selfish of you to walk away without sharing it.

There are free tools that allow you to express yourself like no other generation has been able to do in the past. If you have a business that needs an infusion, then you must engage in social media. If you're seeking a job, and you're frustrated that you're not getting many interviews - then of course, you must engage in social media. If you're unfulfilled, and you're not sure what you're passionate about, leverage social media as a discovery tool. Find like—minded individuals and find your light. You can think about all of the riches you can imagine, you can visualize your dream home, spouse, job — but if you don't act, you have nothing. You can leverage free technology to take action and draw these things to you. Social media is the first step of a global spiritual awakening. This is why so many people fear its power. It's a natural reaction. We're in the midst of the most fascinating, thrilling and inspiring time to be on this planet. Social media and digital connections bring truth to our relationships.

Social media has helped to organize uprisings against oppressive governments and communicated news in a way we never thought possible. We have reconnected with those we'd lost touch with. We have shared ideas and crowd sourced solutions to problems that would have remained unsolved if not for social media.

The better the technology the easier it will be to share with each other. This is the reason why I'm convinced that we're in the early stages of a global spiritual awakening. I believe that human interaction via social media is spiritual. It is a gift to have this technology in our lives. It has allowed us to share ideas, and information faster than ever before in history. This unique interconnection and the resulting network effect is an extension of our collective unconscious.

Embrace this truth, and allow it to set you free when you create content. This is your first step. Let go of the fear, and take that first step. Embrace your truth, yourself, your essence, your being, and share it with the world. Connect with other human beings, add value to their lives. Bring joy, support and love. These are the first days of our awakening together. The Internet has been an integral part of our culture since the late 90s, but only now has it begun to reach its full potential. The idyllic vision for the Internet was to bring human beings together in ways in which we had only dreamt about before. I believe that the Internet will continue to evolve as a vessel for us to communicate with each other. It will allow for near real time dissemination of information (thoughts, comments, updates etc.)...

For now, I want you to have a greater understanding of why social media is so powerful. This understanding will help to guide you in whatever you endeavor in Social Media. If you're blogging and seeking an audience, then you must be true to yourself, and follow your passion. If you are seeking a job, you must put your truth before your desire for stature, and you'll attract the correct job for you. If you are graduating, and you are leveraging social media to discover your dream job, then be honest with yourself in this search. Don't seek the desired role that your mother or father have for you. Search yourself for your joy, your passion, and then discover this company by leveraging the tools I detail in the coming chapters. But only do this if it's your true passion. Social media is only a digital extension of you, no more, no less. Embrace this, and allow for yourself to be open to new opportunity and the joy of your true passion.

While lecturing at Marist College, I naturally followed my truth. I let go of my fear, and allowed the students to see a side of me that I didn't even know existed. I didn't do it on purpose. After reflecting on why speaking there had been so powerful for me, I realized I had allowed my true self to come through because I had nothing to lose. I wasn't standing in front of a potential investor, or trying to win business — and I just wanted to help. What happened was nothing short of magical. I thought I was going to teach the students at Marist everything they needed to know about social media, and guide them to success. But what really happened was the exact opposite.

The auditorium looked as if it could hold a few hundred people, but there couldn't have been more than thirty students. The lights were dim, and I had the stage to myself. I stood just to the side of a ten-foot high screen projecting my presentation behind me. Moments after Professor Timmian Massie introduced me I jerked the microphone from the podium and spent my time oscillating from one side of the stage to the other.

While lecturing, I find it helps to get a few names of the attendees in advance. If I discover something interesting about the person online, I use bits and pieces to illustrate different points. That day was no different, and I included senior Alyssa Bronander in my presentation. I did so, because when I Googled her name, the results included a link to her blog called *Karma Waffle*. The name and content of her blog are inspired by the book *Soulpancake: Chew on Life's Big Questions*. Alyssa's content mostly documents her personal journey through the book. One blog post she added was inspired by a chapter in the book which challenges its readers to spend a day with the oldest person they know. Alyssa took on this challenge, and eloquently blogged about the experience:

"My grandmother is 81 years old and handicapped, having lost the function of the right side of her body in a stroke over ten years ago. For her to be as cheerful and good — humored as she is in her condition is truly inspiring to me. My grandmother has taught me valuable life lessons such as how to make killer rice pudding, that there is always room for dessert, and one should never leave the house without (giant) sunglasses."

Not only did she spend the day with her Gram, she risked ridicule from her college classmates, and put herself out there. Alyssa is fearless. She doesn't care what others think of her post. She impressed me greatly. Why is her example important? As a hiring manager, I may find myself with two resumes on my desk. Both individuals may have a perfect grade point average, and similar extra-curricular activities, however one may be active in social media, and the other may not. Which candidate do you think I'm going to give an offer? Of course there are many factors that effect a hiring decision, however if you've been fearless, and blogged about something as intimate as Alyssa's day with her Gram, I'll better understand what type of person you are. She's now added an additional dimension to her application by allowing herself to be vulnerable. By shedding her façade, she has come closer to her true self, and could potentially draw the right job to her. If nothing else, Alyssa's blog post left me really wanted to meet her in person, and to thank her for showing such grace at such a young age. She shattered my stereotype of college students. She challenged herself, and proved she was raised *well*. It's apparent she respects her elders, and understands what is truly important in life. Can you see why following your truth, being fearless and understanding how social media works can literally change the trajectory of your life?

Similarly I addressed Alyssa's classmate Amanda Huggins in my presentation. After Googling Amanda, I discovered her LinkedIn profile that included her creative work title: "Future PR Powerhouse." When I read this (knowing full well that she was still a student at Marist) I knew immediately that she understands the power of social media. That singular statement told me volumes about her personality. She is serious about her career, and she has faith in her own ability. When I read "Future PR Powerhouse" I believed her!

These students gave me so much more than I could ever give to them. Isn't that how it goes with all the powerful moments in life? Those times become your most humbling moments.

I know that those students no longer view the job search as a linear progression. They see the bigger picture regarding how social media can help them, and showcase not only their talent, but also their humanity. Even more importantly they see opportunity.

Upon returning that night, after telling my wife I would write a book I said, "I would kill to have that feeling every day."

I wrote this book for you. You may be a student looking for a job, or you're unemployed, and ready to make a career change. Or you're sick of your current position, and you want to define yourself in your industry. Maybe you're a stay-at-home parent itching to get back into action again. Maybe you love your job, and you love your company, and you want to tell the world about the new and innovative way the company is run. No matter the case, you're ready to be heard. Let me be as crystal clear as possible. I'm not a sideline pundit that speculates how social media can potentially help people gain employment or their dream job. I've not been handed a family business—I have no inheritance that's been spent on social media seminars. I'm just a regular guy. I've lived it, I feel it and I know it to be truth. I've spent the past four years of my life engaged in social media. By building my own personal brand I landed my dream job, made more money than I could ever have imagined, and eventually found myself appearing in front of millions of people as a social media expert. I never sent a resume to Fox News. I never had media training. I never solicited this huge break. The huge break came to me. It's because I had built a digital reputation so air tight, that when producer Jason Hartelius called me at 2 pm, I was in the studio taping that very evening at 5:30.

It works. You'll need to make adjustments along the way, and that's OK, but the results will be the same. Opportunities will come to you. You'll add value, build your personal brand equity, and make more money than if you rely only on your resume, guaranteed.

The world has changed, and it's up to you to start to harness this power now. This is your time. Your resume is obsolete. So stop tweaking it, and start "thinking" for a change. Showcase your true talent, and engage in social media. Get your butt off the sidelines, and start living.

You aren't here to be mediocre. Mediocrity is a disease that's rampant in our society. I'd bet that nine out of ten of the people who read that statement would agree. "Right on Chris." "You tell em." "Mediocrity stinks." "Go get em" then they'll roll over on the couch, pop on their favorite reality show, and enjoy their down time because they deserve it. Being good at something doesn't cut it anymore.

The only thing you should accept from yourself is to be phenomenal. I don't mean doing something "extra" here and there. I mean being everywhere and *feeling it in your bones. Feel* your business, your job search, your new hobby, your movement, your film, or your book in your soul. Eating, sleeping, and breathing your passion. Sure, you can get a cushy job that will pay well. Why not push yourself? Why not be the best? Why not become a leader? Why not apply for a job at the best company you can find in the industry that makes you salivate? Why not push yourself to learn something new daily? If you hate reading, why not listen to audio books? Why not challenge those books, and write your own. I promise you that the minute you say good riddance to mediocrity, and wholeheartedly live that tenant your life will improve ten-fold, immediately.

Simply doing a decent job isn't only doing you an injustice; it's doing an injustice to the whole of humanity. I don't want to get too "heady" here, but I truly believe this. It's up to you to push yourself, and find out what will fulfill you. Once you do this you'll be happier, and when you finally get to do something and experience true happiness, you'll help to make the world a better place. Do something great.

You'll thank me for it — I promise.

2 LISTEN

"When people talk, listen completely. Most people never listen."

— *Ernest Hemingway*

There is nothing wrong with learning about how to send a Tweet, promote your Facebook page, answer a question on Quora, add a photo on Flickr, or post a video to YouTube; none of it will work however, if you don't listen first. Heck, don't just listen. Listen with every ounce of your being. When I was first learning about social media I did nothing but listen. Even today I read as much as I can. When I'm not reading I'm listening to audio books. When I'm not listening to audio books, I'm picking the brains of people who are much smarter than me. Or is it I? Or me? (Clearly, there are lots of them out there). You'll never grow if you don't consult others. You'll never be able to appropriately engage in social media if all you do is push content. Again, think of the spirituality analogy for social media. The humanity of the actions you're taking in this digital space must be in line with appropriate engagement in life. You'd never just talk *at* someone.

I encourage you to set your social destinations and begin by listening. Ask questions; seek information via numerous resources. Consult blogs, search key words associated with your interests, and read, read, read. Social media is bringing us closer, and allows for information to flow effortlessly. All of this information is there for you. You just have to do is find it. Quiet your mind, define your goals, and seek the information that will further your cause.

Give

On December 14, 2009 my father was told there was a 90% chance that he had a disease call **ALS** (Amyotrophic Lateral Sclerosis). This beast of a disease, more widely known as Lou Gehrig's disease, is a killer. Life expectancy for those afflicted can range anywhere from two to nine years, but eventually it gets you. Immediately after the diagnosis my family hunkered down and braced for a battle. There were no panicked phone calls. Nobody complained, or flew into fits of hysteria. We analyzed our options, and discussed how we would deal with the coming challenges. Friends and family sent emails of support and love. Phone calls and small gatherings with friends showed us all how much love surrounds my Father.

Dad's Reaction: On the third day after the initial diagnosis my Father stoically told my wife Laura and me "it is what it is." Telling us "I don't want your mother to be my care taker; I don't want her to retire. I want her to be my partner." To me, Dad's reaction defined true love. At his darkest moment, my father exemplified grace. Not one word of self-pity. Not one word of dark introspection. I never heard "why me."

Mom's Reaction: My mother calmly explained to me that she believed in the power of prayer. Her father had been given three months to live when my older brother was a newborn. My grandfather went on to live 25 more years. "Miracles are real Chris, believe this." I thought she was in denial. I was wrong.

On December 29th just weeks after his diagnosis, a miracle happened. My father's diagnosis was debunked by specialists at Columbia University. Coincidently, as this was all happening, I'd also just completed reading a book that I highly recommend, *29 Gifts* by Cami Walker. In the book Cami documents her mission to revive the giving spirit in the world. She credits giving with ultimately helping her cope with her multiple sclerosis. She feels that giving changed the way she viewed the world, and altered her energy. I was inspired. With the story of *29 Gifts* fresh in my mind, I decided that I would give 64 gifts, one gift a day for 64 days in honor of my father's 64 years. If I failed to give a gift one of the days I would have to start over. I made it through the full 64 days without missing an opportunity to give a gift. I documented each gift on my blog.

Heartbreakingly my father would eventually be diagnosed with ALS. But those 64 days documented on my blog were nothing short of magic. My experiences were profound. Some days I would give a little to a street musician. Or I would surprise someone and pay for his or her subway fair. One of the most powerful moments came during my normal commute home.

New York City can be an overwhelming place. If you're not accustomed, you will surely be intimidated by the velocity of passing commuters through our subway system. Most visitors wince at the shock of it all. Strong odors, screeching sounds of metal-on-metal pounding the subway rails. As you make your way into the steaming underbelly of swarming humanity, strangers push, shove, and struggle to get by. To them, you're an obstacle, not a human being. Initially, it's terrifying, but eventually you become numbed to the whole visceral experience. As a New Yorker, I don't even think about it. I simply jump into the roaring stream of humanity, and move along my defined route, mindlessly navigating the same path each day. I find solace in the chaos. Trotting along, I become lost in my own thoughts, listening to music, or an audiobook—in my own happy little world. It was while following this normal subway route when I began thinking about my gift for the day. I had decided that my gift would be to one of the many street performers that I encounter on my commute throughout the subway system. At times, I'd hear musicians playing, pause, and pop out my ear-buds out to soak it in. I approached the typical location where I'd seen performers before, but was surprised to find nobody there. Instead I observed a homeless man sleeping on the cold and filthy subway floor. Newspaper served as his primitive blanket. Moving toward him, I had to make a decision. I thought he may be the person to give my gift to, but I really want to get home – no time. A split second later I thought – this guy doesn't have a family to go home to *decision made.* Ducking into the entrance into Grand Central I spotted a small deli selling snacks, sandwiches and drinks. I rushed to the counter, bought a sandwich ($4.25), and turned against the tide of hurried commuters. I didn't want anyone to see me giving him the sandwich. But I really wanted him to know that it was there so he would *eat* the sandwich, so I tapped him on the shoulder. He startled and pulled the newspaper off his face. We locked eyes. I froze, and then found the words "it's a sandwich, enjoy" he blinked as my comment registered. To me, he looked angry I thought I'd made a mistake. I was surprised at what happened next. In a boyishly soft voice he whispered "thank you." I smiled, turned, and followed the tide of humanity rushing home. Because of my detour I was late, and needed to rush to catch the train home. About twenty yards away from the train I heard the familiar signal indicating the doors were about to close, I broke into a full sprint, narrowly ducking onto the train on time. I slumped into my seat and shuddered. I'd just given the most profound gift I'd ever given in my life. I went home and blogged about the experience.

Giving will change the way you view your day. Instead of seeking what people can do for you, you'll start to look for ways to give. This is a powerful exercise in life, not only in social media. I recall the thrill I would feel each day when I would start off to work looking for ways that I could give a gift. Sometimes I'd daydream about what gift I'd give the next day. Giving will change your life. Give in your digital world and you'll reap dividends. I promise.

I didn't always understand the power of giving. This was especially true in my work life. In corporate American we are taught to look out for No. 1. Don't worry about the next guy, step on his neck to get the promotion. Take, take, take or the other guy will take from you. For sure, I did just that throughout the initial years of my career. Though I cringe even writing this I remember that while seeking my first role as a vice president in sales I was close to getting two offers, and I lied. I told each company they were the *only* company I was dealing with. I pushed each hiring manager to produce an offer. I wanted them to battle for me and in the process drive up my price. It worked. The company I eventually decided to join offered me a sixty thousand dollar signing bonus. High financial reward for sure, yet I lost a part of my integrity in the process. I hated every second of the process, and I lost a friend in the process (the executive recruiter). He realized what I was doing, and when he confronted me I selfishly severed ties.

He was just doing his job. Trying to get the best candidate for his client, and I used him. I told him what he wanted to hear until the very end. I should have known that my big vice president role would crash and burn. This was just bad karma, all take and no give. Three days after I started, my new boss was terminated. I had no internal advocate in the organization and I was eventually terminated myself. Chasing money, never works, ever. Looking out for No. 1, will only and always result badly.

I remember sitting in a diner in London when, in the middle of a conversation with an acquaintance he asked me a poignant question. We were discussing our careers and he asked me if I was "fulfilled"... I'd never in my 28 years (at the time) been asked such a question regarding my career. I was stumped. What did he mean exactly? I was director of sales at such and such company working with these fantastic clients, and had done this and that... fulfilled? What did that even mean?

So now I'm asking you that same question. Are you fulfilled? If you're not sure of the answer than I'll offer you a small bit of advice so you can take the first step to fulfillment: *Give.*

Give something of consequence to someone, as soon as you can. I'm not pressing you to give $100 to your brother-in-law. The best type of giving can simply be giving your time and attention. Same goes for the social media ecosystem. Become a servant of the people you encounter during your job search, business promotion, and public relations campaign. End every conversation with, "Please let me know how I can help you." Offer your services. Or offer your professional insight by commenting on blogs — reply to inquiries on Quora, add value via Twitter. Search for the query "Question" answer as many people as you possibly can. Silverback Social, LLC often gives of our time and effort regarding digital marketing. Many people don't have the means to pay us, so we just give them advice for free, or help them to get started. We just recently built a free website for my Cousin Stephanie Dessi Kiley's Occupational Therapy business. It truly feels wonderful. Give until you're blue in the face.

Show your neck

In the fall of 1989 I was playing football at Mahopac High School, and my coach, Ted Georgalas, was in the middle of calling a play. Suddenly he paused looking for words that escaped him. He was at a loss. On the nearby field was Tony Amendola leading our Junior Varsity team.

Older, and with more experience coaching, Coach Georgalas called over to Coach Amendola and asked him a question about the play. He then turned to the team and said "Gentleman, I'm not too proud to ask when I'm not sure." At that moment I was prepared to run through a wall for Coach Georgalas. So apparently was the rest of the team — we went undefeated that season.

Frequently within the world of social media I read of self-proclaimed experts. The bombast, pomp and circumstance make me wince. The snake-oil salesmanship has hurt social media. One of the reasons why Fox television producer Jason Hartelius was drawn to my content and my "personal brand" is because I'd written that anyone who says they're a social media expert is full of crap. The technology changes so rapidly that it's virtually impossible. I wince when I hear someone use the term "guru" to describe a social media pundit. Show the chinks in your armor. Show your neck, and people will be further drawn to your humanity.

Curate your content, be aware of the way you position your personal brand, but don't be afraid to show people who you *really* are. Let them know when you're not sure. Admit that you're learning about a new technology, and ask for their help. Show your neck and they'll realize perhaps that they can help you, and what a wonderful way for a friendship to blossom. As your twitter followers to help you get an answer to a question your boss asked you. You could turn up some amazing findings.

The Playing Field has Evened

The manner in which we aggregate and disseminate information as a culture has changed forever. Six or seven years ago, if you were looking for a job, you'd polish up your resume, craft a cover letter or two, and start pounding the pavement. Sometimes, if you were feeling resourceful, you'd look for an introduction via an acquaintance. Generally you were at the mercy of human resources, whose job involved sifting through the never- ending piles of resumes. You were expected to wait patiently. The chance of your resume landing in the hands of the right person, was, at best, slim. I once read an article where a human resources manager confessed that her boss had not read a cover letter in eleven years.

The old way of gaining employment is dead. This old process has no color, no flavor, and no personality. In short, it has no *you*. Even if there is a company out there that will only accept resumes on a Tuesday and from Ivy

League schools, be aware that every member of the human resources team *will* Google everyone they're preparing to interview because that's the way our culture works. Whether they're conducting an audit on you and your background, or just because they're curious, they'll Google you at some point, guaranteed. You don't live on a piece of paper anymore. So learn to deal with it. And if at first, it seems scary, relax. However, this is the most exciting and important technological development of the past five years. The playing field has been evened! My goal for you is to seize the opportunity. I want you to own your Google results. You can own these Google results by creating a blog and profiles on numerous social media sites, like Twitter, LinkedIn, Tumblr or Quora. After creating profiles, begin to engage with the communities and create content. The content you generate here will bubble up to the top of your search results. When a potential employer Googles you, I want them to gasp. I want them to be utterly and completely mesmerized. I want them to scan the page and immediately know that you are the candidate they need to hire.

They'll be impressed when they see you have thousands of Twitter followers. They'll be even more impressed when they see you've started your own LinkedIn group leading the conversation about your selected industry. They'll also be impressed with your eye contact and camera presence when you video blog. Think of this power. Think of how thrilling it will be to turn these tables? Think about how excited they'll feel when they finally get to meet you for an interview. You have now given them the context to know where your thoughts are. They'll see that you are thoughtful, and that you take your career seriously. Never before have you had the chance to communicate ideas with such ease, and at no cost. There is no reason why you shouldn't engage in social media to gain employment. You now have the ability to create your own personal charismatic brand via digital places. The more content you create in these social spaces the more organic search results that will show up when someone Googles your name. You then have the ability to show the world who you really are. It takes work, and you must generate content regularly, but being able to own these results is inestimable for your career.

It's simple

As a young man attending interviews, I'd scan the office of the person I was speaking to, desperate to find some sort of human connection outside the realm of our conversation. In the final interview for my first job I noticed there was a phrenology bust in the hiring manager's office which kicked off a great conversation (Google it - they're fascinating). We connected. All I'm encouraging you to do is to connect − social media is the modern equivalent of scanning someone's office to find a neutral ground, common interest or link, *context*.

Social media also allows you to spread a message to a vast number of people. They, in turn, can then share that message with like−minded friends. While harnessing the power of social media is not rocket science, however it does it does involve attention to human nature. Believe it or not our grandparents were masters of social media. My friend Gary Vaynerchuk (more on Gary in Chapter 5) uses this anecdote and I love it − when your grandparents walked into the local butchers, the butcher would slice the meat your grandmother was about to order. He knew her by name and how many children she had. The butcher had *context*. Social media offers the same in our "speed of light" society. When I see someone at a conference who I've Tweeted with, I understand who I'm now talking to in person. This is because I have *context*. While content is key within the social media world, I encourage you to explore *context* too.

When you're looking for a job, the human resources manager will have context from the moment you walk through the door. This opportunity to add context to a relationship is extremely powerful.

It also works the other way around. I encourage you to leverage these powerful new tools to learn more about the company you may be interested in working for. Conduct a Google search, learn about the executives, review their LinkedIn profiles, and follow their Twitter profiles. Read their blogs, and study.

3 CURATE STORIES

"Storytelling is the most powerful way to put ideas into the world today."

—*Robert McAfee Brown*

My friend Chris Cornell used to own and operate a framing store called Cornell Gallery. Chris's gallery wasn't the most "blog rich" environment, however I pointed out to Chris that the blogging shouldn't be singularly focused on the framing. Sure, he could always talk about the frames and how they further enhance the photos and paintings. However, I encouraged Chris to approach framing from a different perspective.

When I was 18-years-old my grandfather, or Papa as we called him, wrote me a letter in response to my receiving the Coaches Award during my days as a prep football player. At the time I thought this was nothing more than a "nice" gesture. I put the note in my desk drawer and never thought much about it. When I uncovered the letter as a thirty three-year old, it shook me. Upon reading it I began to cry. I even framed the letter and placed it on my nightstand, it remains one of my most prized possessions. I encouraged Chris to blog about stories such as these. While framing is at the core of the story, it has nothing to do with what Chris' frames offered his clients. He shouldn't have been discussing framing in the social media ecosystem. Instead blogging about the stories and emotion behind the framing. Uncovering "why" people frame certain things is where the real interest lies.

If you have the ability to tell stories, you have the ability to engage in social media. The conversation usually begins with someone telling me they can see the need for social media in their business, or that they think it will help to build their personal brand. This comment is inevitably followed by, "But I have no idea what I would blog about." Truth be told, there is potential blog fodder in every single human interaction. You're communicating a story, suggesting your take on the situation, and giving the person you're speaking to the opportunity for an opinion about the information you provided.

When you have this interaction you're inevitably telling a story. "Did you hear about ...?" "Did I tell you that this happened ...?" What you're really doing is telling stories! If you're a business owner, then engaging in social media is no longer a choice. Whether you like it or not, "social" is happening to you and your brand. The amateur has been empowered with the tools to create content. You cannot control it, but you can engage and participate. As a result you can address and alleviate negative commentary, as well as promote positive chatter. You can take a disgruntled customer who would never again have done business with you and transform him into a repeat customer by expeditiously addressing their issue. And you can turn a relatively pleased customer into a brand advocate by telling him how much you appreciate his praise. Now is the time to engage in social media. Don't hesitate. You have nothing to lose and the whole world to gain.

Can you now see now how blogging on behalf of your business can support not the product you're selling, but rather the culture of your business, and the *real* reason why people buy from you? The *you* of your business.

If you're a student, the ability to experience something, take what you're learning into the classroom, form an opinion, and post it on a blog is the single most powerful thing you can do beyond your grades and campus activities. A high grade point average is great, but if you package those fantastic grades with thoughtful blog posts, and a powerful online identity like Alyssa Bronander, then *real* power is at your disposal.

Don't wait for your commencement speech before you start feeling excited and motivated. Start a Tweetup, and start your own groups right now. You don't have to wait for anyone's guidance, or until you're in a job where you have access to a super computer. Your super computer is your laptop. Most of the services I've mentioned in this book are free. Start *now*!

4 SOCIAL MEDIA MADE SIMPLE

"The Buddha, the Godhead, resides quite as comfortably in the circuits of a digital computer or the gears of a cycle transmission as he does at the top of the mountain, or in the petals of a flower."

— *Robert M. Pirsig*

The *Truth Machine* by James Halprin (in development to be a major motion picture) was recommended to me over ten years ago. In the book, Halprin imagined a time where an infallible lie detector is invented. At first it's implemented on boarders, and used as a law enforcement tool. Gradually it becomes integrated into our everyday lives. As a result, students can't cheat, corporations, and politicians can't lie. We inevitably get smarter. We're forced to actually *learn* what we study. Our relationships become stronger (bound by truth). Companies improve. There are no short cuts; there are no back room dealings. All impropriety becomes impossible because of the truth machine. The first generation that encounters this machine does so with trepidation. They malign the Truth Machine as unnatural, and ineffective. However, as generations pass, people begin to acclimate and evolve; becoming better as a result. The new generation, doesn't know any different. All they know is a world with the truth machine. Truth permeates society.

Social media is a non-fictional truth machine. If you don't embrace the seismic shift that social media has created, you'll be left for dead. There's new generation who have grown up with this technology. Social media doesn't scare them because they don't know any different. They're thrilled to interact, collaborate, and be transparent because they have *nothing* to hide. They're used to interacting this way. They want to get better, create, and be useful.

Playtime is over. Improve your presence in social media today. Make yourself better and don't cut corners. Social media isn't going anywhere. Lie on your LinkedIn profile, and it will come back to haunt you. Slander someone on

Facebook, and it will live in perpetuity. Trust people, and listen- let go. Engage, and thrive.

Now that you understand the essence of social media, it's time to engage in social media. Where you begin depends on your goals and objectives. Which audience are you trying to reach? Where do they convene? Where do they exchange information? Social media destinations may disappear tomorrow. What you need to understand is that the manner in which this information moves has changed. Social media as its structured today is the first iteration of technology assisting our fully connecting via our collective unconscious. There is beauty in this technology.

Those who embrace social media will leverage an accelerant in their personal and business lives. Those who choose to ignore it will be left behind. You must evolve with this technology, or in essence you, your brand, your message, will undeniably die.

The spiritual connection via social media is of course not fully evolved. However, we are seeing some powerful developments being ignited by social media. I do believe that eventually, we will all be connected via technology. I see beauty in the initial flare of human connection amplified by social media. When the seed for change is planted, it can grow at such an accelerated rate that the proverbial playing field had evened around the world. So now a citizen like Wael Ghonim with access to the Internet can spark a revolution.

In June of 2009 Clay Shirky spoke at a (TED) *Technology, Entertainment, and Design* conference. Their website describes them as *"a nonprofit devoted to Ideas Worth Spreading."* Shirky's talk was titled: "How Social media Can Make History." His words were profound.

Clay spoke about how there are only a few inventions over the course of the past 500 years that can truly be labeled as revolutionary. Let's take a look:

Printing Press: I think we can all agree that the printing press was a revolutionary invention. The printing press allowed for mass distribution of information throughout Europe. This allowed for a powerful means of communication. Communicating a message from one to many.

Telegraph/Telephone: This invention allows for one to one communication, communicating over long distances and for the first time there is immediacy to our conversations. We can think of someone, ring him or her up, and then we have this discussion.

Movies/Sound: This invention allows for like-minded groups to convene. There is a shared experience that we've not had before.

Radio/Television: Similar to movies, this media is digested individually, or in groups.   There is a shared experience that brings us closer, and this media is used as outlets for one to many communications.

Internet/Social media – Here's where things change drastically. This is why you must evolve or die. The Internet, or social media – (the further evolved version of the Internet) that we've seen in recent years can do a few things that are revolutionary. Social media not only shares the same characteristics of all the revolutionary developments of its predecessors, it actually envelopes each revolution into itself. So all activities, phone, movie, TV, print, etc. all live *in* social media. One to one becomes one to many, which becomes many to many. This doesn't define the true revolution however. The earthshattering development that serves as the leveler of the field is that the consumer of the media is now *creating* the media. This idea that those who digest media now create media is where things get exciting. Are you ready to own this, and begin to create your own media? Why wouldn't you? It's free. It's powerful, and it's easy.

In 2007 China experienced an earthquake of over 7.0 magnitude in the Chen Chen province. Shirky described that first news of the earthquake came via Twitter. The BBC broke the story as it happened. China's residents Tweeted and shared horrifying images of the devastation.

Back room dealings of corrupt government officials in the province had approved substandard building throughout the city and resulted in a higher death toll that expected. The result was the catastrophic toll on families with children who were in school that day. Schoolhouses collapsed and effectively wiped out a full generation of each family affected because of the one child limit the government has imposed. Parents took to the streets in protest. Images of the corrupt officials lying prostrate begging for forgiveness in the streets were tweeted and shared around the world. These images proved to be too much for the Chinese government who eventually cut off access to the Internet. The Chinese government wasn't ready to censor this type of information because the people generated the content, not by the media covering what the people were experiencing. The media was shared from the inside out.

Home Base

Very early on I realized that Twitter would be a powerful tool for my business reputation. The early adopters on Twitter were businesses people and it was a fertile ground to learn, and establish myself as an authority in social media. I also realized that in order for me to fully communicate the ideas that I'd around business, family, and self- improvement I needed to have a "home base." My blog became my home base, and each social tool became an extension of that home base. Facebook for my friends and family, Twitter for my business, and my blog as the epicenter of it all.

While you may take a different approach, I encourage you to define your social self with this concentric circle structure in mind. It's easier to manage your social places when there is a hierarchy. If you place certain priorities on certain social places you'll be able to manage more effectively. Otherwise you run the risk of being utterly overwhelmed with updates, monitoring and curating content. Define your "home base" and then articulate which social spaces will serve as extensions of your social self.

For example: If you're a start-up jewelry company like Adornia, (with lots of visual components to your product offering), you'd make Pinterest your main hub of activity. YouTube, Twitter, Facebook and your blog would all be extensions of this main profile.

Peddle Downhill

It was the summer of 1986, and I was riding my bike with my big brother Mark. Back then, we had a habit of riding our bikes side-by-side "CHiPs" style down the street. That day was no different. We were on our way to visit the coolest kid on the block, Rich Casciato. We'd just turned onto Rich's street, Brookside Road which was all-downhill. At this point Mark and I would usually glide the rest of the way; happy to sit up – pull our hands off the handlebars and enjoy the warm breeze on our tanned faces. Only this time, as we began to feel the pull of gravity down the hill, I decided I wasn't going fast enough and began to *peddle* downhill. At first my eleven-year-old legs weren't rotating fast enough – I felt no torque from the chain. My legs jerked and yanked at nothing until finally I felt it. As my brother looked on in horror, I stood up and pedaled. I bent forward, my backside up, head down low, determined to push the pace. Mark immediately let me know his unease at my sudden burst of peddling fury. As I broke from formation he panicked. I heard his voice trail off as I pulled away, and continued down the hill "Chris, you don't *peddle* downhill, you *break* downhill." I could barely make out the last few words, but I got the gist. I didn't care, I wanted to peddle. By now the warm breeze had transformed into a wind tunnel — making my eyes tear up. I was peddling as hard as I could downhill. It felt amazing. I was following my bliss, finding my voice, and peddling downhill.

For years I used this story as the definitive tale to articulate the difference between my brother and myself. We're 26 months apart but as we've grown older we've come closer to looking like twins than either likes to admit. So when the question of what differentiates us is posed, this story suits me just fine. I wore the story like a badge of honor for years. I'm the wild one. The right brained one. I'm the one that jumped at the chance to live abroad in Belgium, and took the job in London. I partied too hard, I pushed. Mark is steady Eddie. He plans, he executes, and he has laser focus. He's the attorney; I'm the Internet guy. Enough said.

I always peddled downhill. I never questioned that impulse. It was natural to me, and it served me well until a certain point in my career. But at some point I stopped peddling downhill, and I suffered the consequences. Follow your gut, be true to yourself, listen to the voice inside you and always, *always* peddle downhill.

About three years ago I listened to a podcast of a lecture given by Robert Cialdini at Stamford University. His lecture gripped me. His *Six Universal Principles of Social Influence* helped me to build a fertile Twitter community and I think his principles can help you.

1. **Reciprocation** – In general, people feel obligated to return favors. If you leverage Search for Twitter to find like – minded people, or businesses that are either competitors of tertiary to your industry, I recommend that you follow them. More often than not, they'll follow back, and then you'll have an instant community of Twitter followers who are interested in the same things as you!

2.   **Authority** – We naturally look toward authority figures to learn what to do, when to do it, and how often we should be doing it. Establish yourself and your business as an authority. Blog, post comments on blogs, offer insights, re-Tweet, and generally engage with the Internet community. Over time you'll be regarded as an authority (as long as you truly know what you're talking about).

3.   **Commitment/Consistency** – We want to act consistently with our commitments and values, therefore we like to "play nice in the sand – box." Twitter is not the place to rant and rave. Post a negative comment about your competition and almost certainly it will return to haunt you. Follow the old adage, "Do unto others as you'd have done to you." Similarly if you're interested in building your personal online brand, please refrain from negativity within your social places. Because social media is the first iteration of our collectively unconscious, it can be a powerful accelerant. So based in the law of attraction if you're feeling negative and put negative content out there, you'll expeditiously attract negativity back.

4.   **Scarcity** – The less available the resource, the more people want it. Translation: pace yourself. Nobody

wants to read 500 Tweets a day from the same person. The only people I see getting away with volume Tweets are news outlets. Let your followers look forward to high quality Tweets. Use discretion.

5. **Liking** - The more we like people, the more we want to say yes, and the more likely we are to add you to our #followfriday list, re-Tweet, or generally pay attention to what you're doing. Friends recommend friends, and over time friendships grow. So approach Twitter with the sense that you want to meet people and make friends. If you keep this in mind while you're engaging in Twitter (even if you're a business) your community will grow. If all you can think about is what the Twitter community can do for you, you're doomed. Friends are there to help each other. Don't be a parasite.

6. **Social Proof** - We tend to look to what others do in order to guide our behavior. Don't shy away from publicity that will establish your brand as an authority. If your community loves you, new members of that community will follow suit.

Your World is Exploding

Engaging in social media helps us think about who we are, what we represent, what we're passionate about, and what makes us get up in the morning. For me it's my family, friends, and social media itself. I've been fortunate to leverage tools like Twitter and my blog to find that passion. I knew I was interested in social media, but once fully engaged I was able to examine what I wanted from life, and employ what I'd learned and become truly engaged in the social media ecosystem

Get personal

My full name is Christopher Guy Dessi. I love 80's hair bands, the movie Goodfellas, brunettes, and black Lamborghini's. I hate being shushed, glitter, pleated pants, and math. When I was in fifth grade I passed a note to Danielle Bennett and asked her to meet me behind Lakeview Elementary so I could kiss her. She responded with an enthusiastic – "That's gross." Why am I telling you all this? Because social media is all about getting personal.

Offering *some* insight into your personal life is essential for success in social media. For brands I recommend a "peek behind the curtain"... or some sort of insight into the inner workings of your company. If you have a company softball team, feature it on your Facebook page. If you employ a M.I.T Ph.D., allow her to answer questions on Quora on behalf of your organization. Certainly there are times when getting personal is not advised. Politics and religion for example may lead to more negative than good.

I offer personal information on my blog posts, such as "Open Letter to Papa" in which I discussed how I miss my grandfather. These posts added a layer to my blog that I never expected to be there. Furthermore, blogging has helped me in my business and personal life. It's become a personal journal. I've chronicled my journey through unemployment, exhilarating moments with my family, interesting friends, business decisions, and tidbits of entertainment. I encourage you to take off the filter, and allow for some of your personality to shine through. Open your heart, and allow people to connect. If you're seeking employment and you feel like opening up may be the wrong thing for you, I'd encourage you to take the opposite stance. Now is the most important time for you to open up. The moment an executive reviews a post of your which resonates with him, is when you will get a job offer. I want you to find the core of what makes you tick in these blog posts. The companies that feel your blog posts don't resonate are not the right company for you in any case.

1. **Express yourself**: I'm not a great writer, but maintaining a blog has helped me to develop my writing skills. More importantly I have honed the skill of self-expression. This has only helped to cultivate rich relationships in my life.

2. **Be transparent**: I've been 100 percent honest with everything I post on my blog — good, bad, or indifferent. I've embraced the tenant of transparency in social media, and I've discovered liberation in doing this. It led to some of my most gut — wrenching blog posts while unemployed, or dealing with my father's ALS. I've found that being transparent has proven fully liberating in my personal life too. I've been able to shed any bombast, or inclination to mislead about my place in this world. It is what it is — and it's all out there in the social media ecosystem.

3. **Share ideas and tell stories**: I never realized what a vivid storyteller my Grandpa was. He liked to spin yarns about growing up in Brooklyn that would keep my brother and I sitting captivated at his feet for hours. My grandfather was a phenomenal man of staggering intellect.

He knew that a lecture would fall on deaf ears, but a story entwined with a life lesson would resonate. I've been reminded of this via blogging. You can't just shout your opinion; you need to give context, perspective, and share.

4. **Acknowledge those you love and admire**: Blogging has offered me a platform to "shout from the rooftop" how much I love and admire certain people in my life. I recommend you give it a try. There's no shame in putting some positive energy out there. I've taken great pride in featuring those on my blog who warrant shout-outs. It's always unexpected and always warmly received. The world could use some more positive energy out there, and it will make you feel fantastic. This isn't just a blogging technique; this is a life lesson. Sharing with the world how amazing someone in your life is can be a powerful shifter in your mind and spirit. I often turn to my blog when seeking that unique gift for Father's or Mother's Day.

5 THE CATALYST

"Caring is scalable now."

— *Gary Vaynerchuk*

Some three years ago I was attending the Web 2.0 conference in New York City when I caught Gary Vaynerchuk's keynote. Gary is an immigrant from Belarus, Russia, wine storeowner, digital agency owner, and author of *Crush It* and *The Thank You Economy*. When I heard Gary speak he was just breaking onto the scene. His keynote changed the trajectory of my career. I decided then and there that I would evolve my career into social media. Gary is a fireball of energy that ran onto the stage that night with no power point presentation to back him up. I'd spent the conference hearing some really eye opening presentations. But hearing Gary speak that day about building a personal brand via social media overwhelmed me.

There was something about the way Gary presented his keynote that stuck with me. Gary is very much an "every man" and when Gary came on the stage, I saw myself.

Do you know that feeling when you've tried to sound smart and use a big word, only to be corrected by someone the moment that word left your mouth? Gary seemed to have bottled that very moment into a canister and used it to power the engine that drove his keynote. Gary opened up by telling us how he built his family business from $4 million to $50 million, but when he turned thirty he realized he wanted more from him life so he started WineLibraryTV an online Video blog where Gary reviews the wines he sells in his wine store. Gary built this video blog into a social media empire. Gary doesn't just review the wines on his show. He distills his review so that even a wine neophyte like me can understand his review. He references every day words and experiences and relates them to wine. Instead of saying "I'm getting some oak scent at the back of his palette"....he'll bark "I'm getting serious oak-monster here." For me, *this works.* It also works really well for about one hundred thousand online viewers per night.

At the time of hearing Gary speak I was vice president of sales at a multi-national performance-based ad network—and I was *miserable*. I earned over three hundred thousand dollars that year. I had a prestigious title, but I wasn't fulfilled. Gary spoke from the heart, and I was ready to hear his message. He told simple anecdotal stories, and they made so much sense to me. Hearing him was a flash point. Why hadn't this registered for me before? I was starting to see the digital landscape change, but Gary distilled this information so it was easily digestible. He simplified the information and presented it in such a way that it clicked. After I heard Gary I went home and studied. I wanted to do what Gary was doing. I followed him on Twitter, watched his video blog and generally stalked the guy. A few months later I reached out to Gary to meet with him in person. I wanted to tell him how much his keynote had changed my career. I also wanted to work for Gary at his new digital marketing firm VaynerMedia. I ended up working at Buddy Media, where I would introduce Gary to CEO of Buddy Media, Mike Lazerow. Gary would eventually sit on the board of advisors at Buddy Media. For a short period during my tenure there, our two companies shared office space, and I was lucky to observe Gary in action. I tried to learn as much as I could. Purchase his two books *Crush It*, and *The Thank You Economy*. They'll be invaluable tools as you engage in social media.

Your World is Exploding

6 ENGAGE

"If you're sincere, praise is effective. If you're insincere, it's manipulative."

–Zig Ziglar

In the spring of 2006 my parents hosted the engagement party for my wife Laura and I. In the middle of the party we shared a video that I'd created for Laura documenting our courtship, and culminating in our engagement. I love making these types of videos. I'd made my first back in 2001, and since then I've created videos for birthdays, weddings, engagements, and even St. Valentine's Day. That day was special. I had spent a great deal of time compiling the footage, coordinating with the right music, and making sure I'd included everyone who we'd invited to stand with us as our wedding party. I recall that my parent's den was packed and I happened to be sitting on the floor next to my Uncle Joe. Uncle Joe is my Dad's brother. He's been an educator and coach for the past thirty-five years, and I adore him. He's the consummate coach, and sports fanatic, but he doesn't fit the stereotype of a brutish coach. While he is imposing physically, Joe has a softer, tender side that I aspire to emulate. He has no fear of emotional intimacy, and presents no bombast in any interaction. He's a role model of the truest and highest form.

As the video came to a dramatic climax, Uncle Joe scooted closer to me, gave me a hug and looked my straight in the eyes and said "you bring this family so much joy." I was overcome by his candor, and emotion. He wasn't proclaiming his words from a podium. He had me all to himself. Nobody else heard what he shared with me until now. He didn't make the comment for any other reason than to share his own true feelings at that moment. His words had an intense, profound and deep impact on me. I will never forget the tone of his voice, and the absolute, palpable manner in which he delivered his words.

Today's brands have the ability to engage in a similar manner with their consumers. Gary Vaynerchuk has said

"The key to making money via social media is to stop trying to make money", and instead generate useful content and engage with your community. Generate something that will move your fans. Generate content from an unadulterated, pure place and they will engage with you.

Silverback Social coaches our brand clients to flip the marketing funnel. This idea, first presented by the brilliant Joseph Jaffe in his book *Flip the Funnel: How to Use Existing Customers to Gain New Ones.* Jaffe reminds us that at the top of the funnel, a brand executes print advertising, television advertising, search engine marketing, and display advertising, and toward the bottom of that funnel there may be a conversion event such as a purchase. Many brands make the mistake of placing social media at the top of the funnel and include it in the marketing mix. This is a mistake because social media is all media. There is really no such thing as social media. The idea that social media is something separate from any interaction an company has with their consumer is farcical. To believe that social media should have a separate identity while you're ushering a potential customer to purchase will never work in today's world.

We advise our clients to place social media at the bottom of the funnel, after the conversion event. If you've executed effectively, when you reach your consumers via social networking, those brand advocates will enhance all of your marketing efforts throughout the funnel. In social media you can market to and *through* your happy customers.

Take it a step further and understand that social media permeates every facet of your business. Social media is a cultural shift because of the numerous other technologies at your customer's disposal. Your entire company should be aware of the power of social media, and how to harness that power for each silo within your organization.

Social media is an ideal place for businesses to address any public relations issues that may arise. While engaging in social media on a site like Twitter, if a **PR** issue comes up; your community manager can address the issue almost immediately. You have now turned a **PR** disaster into a **PR** success story.

People leverage social media to be social. When they're on Facebook or Twitter certain customer service issues may arise. More and more customers are tracking down business in social media because they expect you to be there. They'll seek out someone at your company and expect to be addressed. If you have a community manager dedicated to listening and addressing issues, it can turn someone into a brand advocate almost immediately.

If your customer finds value from either following you on Twitter, being a fan of your Facebook page or installing your Facebook application, they'll only become more "brand loyal." Bring something to the table, and you'll reap the rewards.

There has never been a better time for research and development. If you listen closely you'll glean priceless information from your user base. They'll offer insights that no focus group would ever offer. You have fully engaged brand advocates who want you to be better. If you listen to them, you can open lines between your customers that have never before been opened.

While engaging with your customers or followers you can also leverage social media to exchange ideas with others in your industry. Social media can serve as an ongoing, fertile "conference." Engage with competition and learn.

Once you start to engage with your community via social media, don't stop there. Generate content that's original and appropriate, ask for opinions and feedback, and always be available. Define yourself as a thought leader.

Twitter is great if it's used properly, but I cannot stress enough that you have to be careful, and not fall prey to "jamming promotions" down people's throats. It's OK to offer "Twitter only" coupon codes, and limited promotions via your Facebook page. These tools can be very powerful but only after you have appropriately engaged that community. Otherwise you'll drive them away.

Get involved and engage with your consumers, but do so with some thought concerning your goals and objectives. Leverage tools that are free to listen to the community: Google Alerts, TweetDeck, Social Mentions, RSS, Radian 6. You have nothing to fear, and *everything* to learn. What do people *really* think about your brand/product/management? Iterate appropriately.

Create benchmarks to help you outline your social media strategy and start measuring audience, engagement, loyalty, influence, and action.

Be Discoverable

When I was 10-years-old, I played on a baseball team. I wasn't a shy kid, but I wasn't especially confident in my abilities. I complained to my dad that none of the kids on the team even knew my name. I didn't go to school with any of them, so I felt like an outsider. Despite this, I loved playing baseball—and my coach gave me ample opportunity to shine.

One afternoon, I realized I was missing my dad. He worked long hours and had trouble attending some of my games. It was a sunny afternoon and as the seventh inning began I stood in the on-deck circle. Then—my dad showed up. He had rushed straight to the game from the train station and was still wearing his office suit! I couldn't have been happier. He passed me a piece of cinnamon trident, and encouraged me to swing away. "Hit it just like we practiced in the backyard," he said. I made my way to the plate and smashed my first home run. Afterward as we walked back to the car, Dad said "I think they know your name now." This lesson was striking.

In business, as in life, there's a time to be noticed. Now, more than ever, social media allows you, as an individual executive, to be noticed. Imagine if I'd hit that home run and nobody was there to witness it? That's the equivalent of knowing your business, but not sharing your knowledge with your community.

When developing your personal brand, keep it simple, unique, and focused. Provide great content and express your unique opinion on topics associated within your area of business. Be unique in the content you generate. For example, find posts about your industry, then offer your opinion in a blog post. Focus on your area of expertise and own that niche. Become a thought leader, and position yourself as such.

Once you've set up your social places, make sure you use services such as Networked Blogs, or Hootsuite so you have some scalability and you can post content to several social places at once if you have to. Offer great content via your social places, and track the interactions with your content by leveraging these free tools.

Recently, while compiling a presentation for a senior executive looking to boost his social media presence, the team at Silverback Social came across the perfect case study for a personality who is doing social media the correct way.

Richard Branson is a dynamic personality and CEO of Virgin. He leverages his personal site as the central hub of all his social media activity. He has a strong presence on his blog, Twitter account, and Facebook page. Each of these social places link to the others, and it's very easy to follow him, and to share the content he provides. He ensures that he owns his personal brand, and he allows his followers to discover his content via numerous outlets.

When I was offered the opportunity to "like" content on his site, it posts to my Facebook friends. This is an excellent execution of the Facebook Open Graph. When my friends see this link it functions as an advertising unit for Richard. This is free advertising for him, and it serves as a creative way for him to cultivate additional followers. Chances are that if I've "liked" his content, some of my like- minded friends on Facebook will "like" the content too, with the potential to snowball into a thriving community of likeminded followers interested in Richards's content. Think of the implications this will have on any personal brand. You don't have to spend money on advertising units— you simply have to create content that you feel will resonant within your community.

Charismatic Personal Brand

Barry Libert, author of *We Are Smarter than Me: How to Unleash the Power of Crowds in Your Business* spoke at a Web 2.0 conference and walked the audience through a powerful story about a fictional executive. It went something like this: Most people don't realize the power that comes with creating a charismatic personal brand. They realize they need to "do" social media, only their efforts tend to be disjointed and lack the management brought to their chosen profession. Now is the time to change this. Barry introduced an example. In the presentation he called the person Joe. I'll do the same. Joe is a charismatic executive in a major corporation. He cares about making money, and ensuring that his bottom line is in good shape. He's a phenomenal orator, and has a loyal team of executives that he directs. However, now Joe has hit a wall. He has always been a good listener. Now he's starting to realize that he may have been listening to the wrong people. While his team is talented, they understand they need Joe in order to thrive in their business, so sometimes they tell him only what he wants to hear. Joe doesn't listen to his community of consumers and this has turned into a bigger issue than ever. Today, the community has access to social networks, blogs, and technology to enable them to communicate about any level of dissatisfaction. They could communicate about how much they love Joe's company, but they have nothing to chat about. They want to open a dialogue with Joe, and although he's interested in their feedback, he's not certain how to facilitate that conversation. Just as this community has resources, and free technology to communicate about Joe's company, so does Joe himself. He's just not sure where to start. So what's the solution?

Joe needs to create and cultivate his charismatic personal brand by leveraging the power of social media. Joe, as an executive of a company, is in a position to take a few simple steps. He should create a blog, a Twitter account, and a business Facebook page. He can also create a LinkedIn profile or group, together with a YouTube account. These outlets will ensure that Joe's content will be both distributable, and discoverable. His blog will serve as the center hub of all his communication.

As the leader of his organization he can leverage the blog to discuss his true passions, and to help his community understand him better. Joe is successful so people want to know how he achieved this, and what drives him.

The key to this solution is for Joe to generate unique and interesting content. When faced with this fact most people tend to think, "Why would someone want to know where I am, or what's on my mind," but the truth is they *do*. They want to understand you better. Think about how powerful it would be if Joe, who is traveling to Los Angeles on business, Tweets to his followers that he'll be in L.A. One of Joe's business associates who he hasn't spoken to in years sees this Tweet, and reaches out to Joe to set up a time to meet. This would not have happened had Joe not set up his social community. While Joe may think no one is interested, he's wrong, and he may be missing an opportunity to interact with his peers.

So when Joe creates a blog post, it posts to his Twitter account, and Facebook page. It also allows him to track the interactions associated with his content, and offer him guidance regarding what types of content resonate with his social community. Joe can now generate more content that will resonate with his followers.

The main idea Joe is missing is that he can leverage social media to amplify his message. Secondly he's missing the appropriate social tools to help him listen to his consumers. Joe is great at speaking, but when he communicates his message it only finds its way to a few ears. Joe's communication strategy is not merely flawed. It's antiquated.

By leveraging the appropriate social places, and creating distributable content that is discoverable not only by his employees, but his customers as well, his message would look very different. Once the message reached his customer, they would be able to share it with their network, effectively amplifying every word he created, and creating a dialogue between Joe and his community. This communication is the gem of social media. Joe would then learn about how to improve his product offering, and where his team is doing both a good—or bad —job.

Right now there aren't many individuals or companies willing to take this "risk" of gleaning feedback, which I believe is a missed opportunity to improve upon your product. If you have the appropriate social media governance in place you'll realize you can control the message in social and allow for true sharing to occur. Convene the group, but let go of control, and watch the magic happen.

7 START NOW

"You may delay, but time will not."

—Benjamin Franklin

It's simple to engage in social media. The real issue is whether you are engaging appropriately. Whether you're an individual or a business you need to start by wrapping some management around your social media endeavors. At Silverback Social we create content calendars on behalf of our clients. Taking the time to map out the content, as well as its frequency will pay dividends. Your followers will expect to see your walls posts, and they'll seek your insight. We also make sure that the "type" of content is defined – solicitous content, conversation starters, thought leadership content, etc. It will help when you share the content calendar internally so everyone is aware of what information will land in your social places.

Social media is a qualitative endeavor, but you can add some quantitative data to help you to learn. Leveraging services such as Hootsuite will help. Make sure you track your Tweets, and Facebook posts. Analyze the data and see what resonates with your community. Services like Hootsuite will help you to generate fantastic reports. Don't be afraid to ask your community what type of content they want. If they're fully engaged, and they trust you, they'll offer guidance. Produce content that resonates on a human level, and don't be afraid to write from the heart. We're all human beings, and it's OK to show some vulnerability. Let the community know when you've made a mistake. Acknowledge a complaint immediately, and let the community know that you're working on a resolution. People will understand, I promise. Have some fun with this. Creating content is a blast. You love your brand, and you love what you do. Share why by telling your community why you get out of bed in the morning. Let them know what ignites the passion in you. Chances are that they feel the same way.

Think "behind the scenes," and generate content that your community wouldn't see anywhere else. They'll love you for it. While chatting with my Uncle Bill about what he should write on his blog about, I encouraged him to discuss the travels he had taken throughout his career. I mean, the man has gone everywhere from Brooklyn to Bangkok. I'm sure there is a young executive out there (myself included) who will be inspired by his posts. Show people how things work. What you think is mundane may be exhilarating to someone else. Jason Hartelius is a producer at Fox TV, who isn't impressed himself with much in TV because he's been doing it for so long. But when he gave me a tour of the control room at Fox TV I felt like a 10-year-old. The same goes for Brian Vastano at Steiner Sports. He gave me a tour of their factory and I was euphoric. He had been there often, and didn't think much of it. Imagine if he posts blogs about the new content, or if the producer blogged from the control room during a live broadcast —compelling!

Don't focus only on your business. Recently I received a comment on my blog that I didn't publish. The person was annoyed that I'd blogged about my daughter on a business blog. I don't regret posting personal content here, because at times those posts get the biggest readership. They also tell my readers who I am, and what I value. I guarantee that this is a key factor when one of my potential clients is considering hiring me. People want to work with people they like. So let your guard down, and be human.

8 BE CURRENT

"Leadership involves finding a parade and getting in front of it."

—John Naisbitt

Last Christmas, I had spent three grueling hours battling the holiday rush at the mall. I was hugely unsuccessful at finding a gift for my wife, and had started to get discouraged. I decided to enter one last store before I gave up for the evening. As I dragged myself into the store, I noticed the saleswoman had just given herself a paper cut. I joked with her and shared my theory that a paper cut is more debilitating than a broken bone. She was pleasant, helpful, accommodating and frankly helped me greatly. I found my gift, and had a fun conversation. So, moments after I left, gift in hand, I tweeted about it to over 6000 followers of mine.

As I said earlier, whether you like it or not, social media is happening to your business. Right now, someone somewhere is Tweeting about the crappy service they have just received at an auto-dealership, or updating their Facebook status about the phenomenal new product they bought at Target (telling all seven hundred of their friends with one click). Someone is listening to an unsigned band via a media player – for free. They're downloading content on Bittorrent, or finding a job on Linkedin.com.

If you have time to care about your business, you have time for social media. Get started today. I promise you, it will change your business forever. Set up your blog, add some photos to your posts, link appropriately throughout your blog, and then the fun part...getting a steady readership.

Add comments on leading trade publications with links back to your blog. Start with some research. Conduct a Google search on your topic of interest. In my case I would search for "social media" and review all leading publications. Read all the content and start adding comments. Try not to add vague commentary such as "great post," as this could be viewed as spam, (and is generally frowned upon). Think deeply about your response. Read the post, and add your own angle on the topic. This way your link isn't only solicitous, it's also useful for the reader. You can create a profile on the social site Disqus.com and present the response as your company or as an individual with links to your other social spaces.

Contact thought leaders to guest blog on your site, or vice-a-versa. There are bloggers out there who may have a different rub on certain topics, and if you're interested in creating an environment for true learning for your readers, it can't hurt. You may also want to generate revenue on your blog by leveraging tools like Google AdSense. Google defines AdSense as "a free, simple way for website publishers of all sizes to earn money by displaying targeted Google ads on their websites." The more traffic you can get to your blog, the better.

Review Google's "Trends" daily and find an angle on your content based on trending stories. This is a new one that I've just begun to investigate by reviewing trends, and adding a social media angle to each story. Chances are that there will be traffic to your blog based on the trend. Don't reach for content; however, as if the topic doesn't dovetail with your voice, it will be obvious. I discovered the dramatic events that led up to Clay Duke's suicide this way.

Clay infamously entered a school board meeting in Florida armed with a pistol. Duke held the school board members at gunpoint. He eventually fired on the board members, miraculously not hitting any of them. After exchanging gunfire that injured a security guard Duke turned the gun on himself and died on the scene. At first it didn't seem like there was a social media aspect to this grisly story, however the further I read the more I realized what a powerful part social media played in the story because Mr. Duke had left a suicide note on his Facebook page.

Speaking about hot trending stories will assist you to receive traffic to your site. As I write this, a hot trending topic is holiday shopping. If I want to jump on this wave of traffic I could blog about the different ways people are leveraging social media to receive deals via widgets, Twitter feeds, Groupon, LivingSocial, Facebook page wall statuses, etc.

Link your blog to your Facebook page, and your Twitter feed. I've already mentioned this one a few times, but for the busy professional it's key. Leverage a service such as Networkedblogs to push your content out to all your social places when you publish. This will expedite the sharing of your content and ensure you don't miss a thing. Blog regularly and your readers will begin to trust your content, and share your blog posts by re – Tweeting them, etc.

Here's a great example of how I leveraged Google Trends, and discovered a fantastic story to blog about. On Dec 13, 2010 Chipotle was a white-hot trending keyword on Google. I read the articles regarding what had transpired, and then offered my opinion. I gleaned readership by picking up on a trending story, and adding my thoughts. This technique is invaluable. Here's part of the post:

Chipotle's Cat Debacle:
5 Lessons for Social media Marketers

Faster than you can say Domino's Pizza Debacle, there's a new food chain with a social media mess unfolding. According to AllFacebook.com Chipotle's Mexican Grill is in hot water tonight:

Chipotle Mexican Grill claims on its Facebook page that a hacker approved a post on an employee's page saying she ran over a cat. We have obtained a copy of the original thread that has since been deleted.

Both the employee and the company have posted the same statement on their respective profile and page. The version on Chipotle's page has garnered hundreds of likes and direct replies that continue as we post this:

Fascinating, kind of funny, and a bit off- putting (I'm not a cat person), but who wouldn't express remorse if they ran over a cat? Yikes.

I received a windfall of readership and comments on this blog post. Most of these stories unfold in a similar fashion. Something happens that is a bit off-putting, but far from tragic. Then the media storm hits. So what can we learn from these incidents in social media?

When there are pages with a critical mass of followers who have "liked" the brand, they'll expeditiously police the social space. Even after Chipotle announced that the employee's account had been hacked, someone posted the name and address of the guilty party.

Even if you don't have an answer to the issue, address the community. Acknowledge the problem, and indicate that you're doing your best to resolve it. Even if you have no idea how to address the issue, people must know you're aware of it. It took Chipotle 24 hours to realize the slip. It was long enough to do some serious damage, and cause an uprising by cat lovers who didn't believe the "hacker" story.

Remain calm. These things have a tendency to blow over, as long as they are handled properly, but do take it very seriously. If left unchecked, the issue will take on a life of its own, and if you're found to be in the wrong there will be movements against your company. For instance, this could have blown up in Chipotle's face if it turned out that they hadn't really been hacked. Very quickly there was a "Chipotle Serves Cats" Facebook page with 86 fans.

Tell the truth. Social media is the ultimate bullshit meter. If you bluff—someone, somewhere will find out and then they'll start a Facebook page about it.

Social media is changing the way we digest media. On Dec 15, 2010 Clicker, the complete guide to Internet television, announced that it would integrate with Facebook to further enhance its recommendation engine. This was a pivotal announcement for Facebook — yet another step toward Mark Zuckerberg's true vision of — enhancing your life by knowing what your friends are up to. Zuckerberg feels (and I agree) that the Internet can be a lonely experience. Individuals bounce from one site to the next all by themselves. As these sites integrate Facebook the experience will no doubt be richer and more fulfilling. For example, when I logged onto Clicker, it revealed a list of my friends who "like" shows that I love, such as 30 Rock. How cool is that?

Think of it this way: If you visit your favorite restaurant, that's a fantastic experience. And what if you knew that one of your old school friends was sitting on the other side of the restaurant — would that improve your experience? But what if you knew that four of your friends had visited the same restaurant and had similarly fantastic experiences there? This is hugely powerful for both your experience, and for the particular restaurant. Facebook feels that these experiences are already happening. You may have missed the opportunity to learn that your friend was interested in the same restaurant because you weren't aware that your friend had eaten there. Now we are able to make that connection.

Clicker had already done a great job of recommending shows for you to view based on your likes and dislikes. Now they have integrated Facebook, you can see which of your friends are interested in the same shows, and discover new shows based on their interests. Again, this is very powerful.

After reading this news on Mashable, a social media news blog, I looked at Clicker and they immediately made recommendations based on my "likes" on Facebook. This is another compelling illustration of why Silverback Social continually encourages clients to have a presence on Facebook. If one person "likes" your brand, chances are that many more friends will like it as well. The snowball effect is becoming easier, as Facebook integrates with more companies such as Clicker.

CASE STUDY: PANDORA

On Dec 13, 2010 I was in the middle of one of those days where you slip on your headphones and get all the sundry items that have piled up on your to-do list completed. I'd just started to really dig into things when the same ole' songs appeared — songs by Coldplay, U2, and Springsteen, all artists I love, all artists that on that particular day just made me yawn. I needed something new. I'd been hearing people chirp about a company called Pandora so I decided to check them out. Pandora started in 2000 as part of the Music Genome Project. Teams of musician-analysts listen to music for your benefit. They set out on a mission to group the music they were listening to. They use a few standards to help define a type of music. These standards include melody, harmony, instrumentation, rhythm, vocals and lyrics. It would stand to reason then, that if you like one type of song, they may refer another song with a similar melody, harmony etc., and you'll enjoy the song they recommend. The result is an eerily accurate determination of your taste in music. Better than any mix tape your ex ever made you, Pandora seems to read your mind and peg your taste in music in a simple elegant interface. You can create a musical "station" based on your tastes, and enjoy the ensuing free streaming music. I was immediately addicted. I love listening to music while I work, and Pandora has become my perfect work mate. So I tweeted about the service quickly after I began using it.

@cdessi I may be the last one to the party after "discovering" @pandora_radio today...LOVE IT

The next day a Pandora employee named Aaron responded to my Tweet:

@pandora_radio Welcome Chris! Enjoy the music. - Aaron

My love of the Pandora service isn't what compelled me to add this case study. It's that Pandora was *listening*. After I posted my Tweet proclaiming my undying love of Pandora, not only was Aaron listening, he responded to my Tweet in front of his 50,000 followers! I then tweeted a response to my 6,000+ followers. Now I'm gushing about my experience in this book. By simply listening Aaron created a ripple effect for his brand.

Your World is Exploding

Good for Pandora, good for me, and now, if you've never heard of Pandora - good for you.

9 EMBRACE YOUR INNER GEEK

"I think I've been able to fool a lot of people because I know I'm a dork. I'm a geek."

—*Gwen Stefani*

When it comes to 1980's hair bands, I am a geek. Mötley Crüe, Warrant, Def Leppard, — you name the band, I'm pretty sure I can recite every lyric from every album they've ever produced. When I say "geek" I'm not referring to your inner "nerd." That's a whole different chapter. Your inner geek is the part of you that you cannot deny. Everyone has an inner geek, but not everyone can tap into it. It's that part that only your closest friends know about. For me, it's those 80's hair bands like Whitesnake, and Skid Row. The songs are inextricably linked to my adolescent years. When that music comes I lose control. So when I say "embrace your inner geek," I'm really asking you to harness your passion, and be "OK" with that.

As I mentioned earlier, my Uncle Bill has traveled the globe. He spent 20 years as an engineer at General Electric. They operate in more than 100 countries. At times I believe he visited all 100 offices. Throughout his journeys he encountered people who were interested in chatting on the plane ride. Instead of becoming the victim of their mundane chatter, he devised a line of questioning that would keep them both entertained. He'd start by asking, "What is the one thing that nobody, or few people know about you that you're passionate about?" The answers were oft fascinating. A full-figured female CEO had a passion for ballet. She and her husband even had a ballet barre installed in the bedroom. A barre is a stationary handrail that is used during ballet warm up exercises. Another person was passionate about 50's do-wop. It eventually helped catapult him into a career as a record executive.

This line of questioning stuck with me, and I find it fascinating. Rarely do we ever truly embrace this part of our personalities. Intuitively Bill knew that when someone speaks from the heart, they are always fascinating and unique. I encourage you to follow your passion, embrace your inner geek, and talk about whatever gets your motor running. I still have passionate feelings toward the 80's rockers who helped to shape my adolescence. So while seeking out and icon to help illustrate a point regarding social media on my blog, I sought out someone who greatly interests me: Bret Michaels, lead singer of the 80's glam band Poison.

I love Bret Michaels. There, I said it. Back in 1988, as I said, I was into all kinds of heavy metal and hard rock. I also loved Metallica, Guns 'n' Roses, Van Halen, AC/DC, and Ozzy Osbourne. The louder and more testosterone-charged the music, the more I loved it.

But then there was this softer "poppier" version of the music I banged my head to. Michaels and his Poison band mates wore make-up, but not the scary kind like Kiss. Poison had this odd androgyny thing going. But there they were bouncing around the stage singing *Talk Dirty to Me*, and *Unskinny Bop* - I was hooked. When I was in 8th grade I went to see Poison, perform in Hartford Conn. with two of my best friends, Mike Fennessy, and Steve Singlak. Steve's dad drove us there, and hung out in the parking lot while we enjoyed the concert.

Your World is Exploding

The lights dimmed, the crowd roared, and Poison finally took to the stage. First song, first chord, and I was on my feet pumping my fist. They played the famed opening riff to "Talk Dirty to Me" and I was in rock heaven. I mean, I was seriously into it. I wanted to *be* Bret Michaels.

My section didn't stand up until Bret turned to the nosebleeds on the right side of the stage, pointed to me (well, I assumed it was to me) and proceeded to pump his fist to the music. At this point I was out of my mind, screaming the lyrics and jumping up and down. The whole section had leapt to their feet, C.C. Deville their Brooklyn born lead guitarist was rocking'... Bret was doing his thing, and all was good with our 1988 Hot Tub Time Machine moment. From then on Chris Dessi would love Bret Michaels for life. It's OK, because my wife, along with 99.99 percent of anyone I've ever spoken to for more than three minutes, knows this about me.

Let's review two opposing scenarios and we can decide together which is more powerful:

1. Rock star connects with audience member with a look. Point, fist pump together = fan for life.

or

2. Rock star doesn't look. No point, no first pump together = innocuous hair band wiped from my mid- pubescent memory.

In each scenario "*something*" happened:

1. Personal connection to the kid in the last row = *good.*
2. No personal connection to the kid in the last row = *bad.*

So what the heck does all of this have to do with social media? When Bret's Twitter account first came to my attention I noticed that his last three Tweets that his handlers had synced up with his Facebook account start with the term "Come to"...

* *Come to "Bret Michaels LIVE @ Viejas Casino in Alpine, CA" Friday, October 22 from 7:00 pm to 10:00 pm....*
* *Come to "Bret Michaels LIVE @ Casino Nova Scotia in Halifax, NS" Saturday, October 9 from 7:00 pm to 10:00 pm....*

Your World is Exploding

- *Come to "Bret Michaels LIVE @ Casino Nova Scotia in Halifax, NS " Friday, October 8 from 7:00 pm to 10:00 pm....*

Obviously Bret Michaels is super charismatic. His resurgence into the mainstream is testament to that. He has the "it" factor times ten. He dated lusty women on a silly reality show. He has two gorgeous daughters. He won Celebrity Apprentice after he spent weeks in the hospital recovering from a brain hemorrhage. This is the time for Bret (or Bret's handlers) to leverage the heck out of social media by showing his human side that people gravitate to. Let him connect with his fans the way he connected to a kid in the nose bleeds back in 1988.

If I were handling his account I would allow for Brett to be himself via Twitter. I would show him how to use it, and give him some tips. Or, if he's that busy, I'd sit there and tell him what people are saying on Twitter and let him say what to reply back. This would help this aging rocker propel his waning career back into the stratosphere. Pushing out innocuous concert updates = aging rock star oblivion. Engaging with the Twitter community = Rock star. PS., I love Bon Jovi and Cinderella too!

10 OWN YOUR GOOGLE RESULTS

"Breathe. Know that the Internet has no eraser."

—*Liz Strauss*

When it comes to business, my uncle is one of my heroes. My father is, and always will be my number one influence when it comes to my career but my uncle brought the sizzle to the steak. When I was growing up Uncle Bill was always flying in from someplace I only ever read about in books. He has traveled the world, and he has had a long and storied career. His travels inspired me to spend a year abroad at Katholieke Universiteit Leuven, Belgium while attending Loyola University, Maryland, and later in my career inspired me to take a job in London.

Your World is Exploding

We got talking about one of my appearances on Fox Television. I didn't know this previously, but Bill had appeared on television a few times, mostly overseas. We discussed our experiences, social media, blogging, Twitter, and Facebook. We finally landed on the idea of owning your Google search results. I shared with him the cautionary tale of Ernie Anastos the local news anchor that had interviewed me on a few separate occasions on Fox News. If you've ever watched the nightly news, you certainly know the type. Ernie is a throwback of journalistic integrity and class. He's an old school, hugely talented Emmy award-winning anchor. But if you're not from the tri-state area it's unlikely you'd know who Ernie is, but you may have seen him on YouTube. During a bit of innocuous on – air banter Ernie meant to say "keep on plucking that chicken" he fumbled and said "keep on fucking that chicken," instead. Stop laughing.

The flub has become a viral Internet sensation. Now when you search for Ernie Anastos you won't review the philanthropic work he does off the air, or hear of the awards he's accumulated. You'll instead see the comedic reactions of Ernie's colleagues Dari Alexander, and Nick Gregory as they digest what they heard coming out of Ernie's mouth, live on the air. He's written children's books, and he is active in and around the New York area. The attention gleaned from this slip up has soiled his reputation. The viral spread of the clip has flooded the Google results page for "Ernie Anastos."

After my first appearance I penned a blog post about the legendary journalist. Of course, as I always do with my posts, I added the appropriate key words, added links, and ensured that I shared the post with my followers on Twitter, and Facebook. The weeks following my first on air appearance, if you conducted a Google search for Ernie Anastos, my blog post was the first result. Now, this is no longer the case, however I was the top result for long enough to make a difference. Ernie has won 28 Emmy Awards and nominations, and was nominated for the prestigious Edward R. Murrow Award for excellence in writing. His resume includes too many accolades to list here. He has been in broadcast journalism for close to forty years, yet this one gaff defines him.

I shared this story with my Uncle, and discussed how, if Ernie wanted to really own this organic Google search results, all he needs to do is generate content he *wants* people to see. He will never be able to control the viral spread of the video via YouTube, but he can actively produce content that is properly linked to outside blogs, appropriately tagged, and discoverable to combat the onslaught of inappropriate results. Eventually he will push the unwanted content lower on the results page.

In order to better understand why keywords are important when you generate unique content you should always consider that there are two visitors to your blog or website. There are the people who will discover your content, and there are the spiders that crawl or sift through the code on your site. These spiders generate the result we see in search engines. So if Ernie were blogging great content daily, he'd potentially own the entire first page of his organic Google results without spending a dime. This may seem arduous at first, but if Ernie and his team are constantly generating content he wants to be discoverable, the implications are powerful. The human behavior hasn't changed, but the technology is moving at the speed of light. Move with this change, or die.

After you read this book, I want you to conduct a Google search for yourself. I know it's a bit vain; but it's essential if you want to build your personal brand. No matter what you've achieved in your career, it'll mean nothing if you're not discoverable. Being discoverable means you'll have to sit down, and recall anything and everything you've ever done that you're proud of, and that you want people to see. If you've spoken at a conference, find out where you can gain access to the video footage. Once you have access to this information, it's now up to you to ensure the information is located someplace you can control the manner in which it's formatted, and presented.

On my personal blog I have a page that lists all of my television appearances. It explains each appearance, what was discussed, and then features the content from the Silverback Social YouTube account. I have pulled the video content using software called Snag-it from the Fox site, and put it on my company's YouTube channel, effectively allowing me to "own" the content I've created. When I drive viewers away from my blog they'll end up in a community my company owns on the YouTube channel. I don't have to worry about broken links if Fox decides to pull the videos, or if they move the content on their site. I can control the message on our YouTube channel that features my appearances on Fox TV. We effectively own the entire process, and we provide numerous ways for potential prospects to reach us. Also, we have set our Google search keywords to serve an ad for Silverback Social if someone searches for my name, driving those people to our corporate Silverback Social site. We recommend you do the same.

11 VAN GOGH & SOCIAL MEDIA

"Accomplish the great task by a series of small acts."

—*Tao De Ching*

Tweets alone mean nothing: together, they're everything. By now we all know what a horrible first impression Twitter makes. Some brands and most individuals don't know where to start. They're not certain what to do. They're shocked when they don't end up with hundreds of followers, and completely underwhelmed by the results—they come to Silverback Social and ask, "Why is Twitter valuable?"

Twitter is a listening tool. Value lies in following people with interests that surround your brand, and which your brand advocates. Really listening to what these people are

Tweeting about will help you define your brand's engagement strategy. Really listening could help you define new product segments, and define trends as they emerge.

So, if you're a involved in the culinary arts like Shamane's Bake Shoppe, in Boulder, Colorado, and you specialize in creating wedding cakes as well as serving Boulder's Best Pies, quiches, and cupcakes, (my favorite), you would follow anyone tweeting about weddings, birthdays, or parties... and then listen. Read their Tweets, and see what's on their minds. Search for key words that define your business and start to engage with the people who are tweeting content using those words.

While each Tweet you see from these individuals can seem like mundane chatter, it's actually the *real* power of Twitter at work. What are they reading? What cities are they traveling to? Who or what influences them?

Imagine that you're viewing a gorgeous Van Gogh painting. You're up close and studying each brush stroke. Alone these brush strokes seem like nothing. However, if you take a step back to view the bigger picture, they (like Tweets) start to offer something greater. Viewed in aggregate these Tweets begin to paint a picture. This "ambient awareness," in my view, is the real power for brands on Twitter. You're tapping into the "small talk" or "water—cooler" chatter of thousands of people who you're interested in hearing from.

Tweets tell a story. Listen closely enough, and the story could mean everything for your next product offering, the new direction for your brand, or even help you to define a new market.

A few years ago I finished listening to a fascinating audio book called *Crowdsourcing: Why the Power of the Crowd Is Driving the Future of Business,* by Jeff Howe. I can't stop thinking about the implications of this theory within the ecosystem of social media.

In the book, Howe explores the rise of the amateur, and how today, more than ever, individuals can participate in an activity they love at a fairly high level. He cites an example with birdwatchers. Amateurs defined a new species of bird a full year before the professional community announced the discovery.

Power is shifting. Tools are readily available to everyone. Websites don't cost what they used to. People can publish and share information easily with the click of a mouse. It's only natural then that professional communities who aren't embracing the power of crowd sourcing are failing when those that welcome it are blossoming. NASA put crowd sourcing to the test by leveraging their internal experts to conduct a test that took two years. They documented their findings, then offered the test to the community and waited. So, what was the result?

In less time, for less money amateurs solved the problem; coming up with the same conclusion as NASA's "professional" team. Fascinating, don't you think?

So why does this work, and how can these make our society smarter? Apparently a crowd will always outperform an individual, and here's why: think of the "Who Wants to be a Millionaire" scenario. The audience is almost always right. If there's a difficult multiple-choice question that nobody knows the answer to, odds are that people will guess evenly across each of the four options. If only one soul in the audience knows the answer, the crowd is correct. Again, I find this fascinating.

Apparently the crowd gets more intelligent when the individuals become more diverse, and this holds true in jury selections, game show studio audiences, and anyone with a passion for bird watching who can share their finding with the global community. Here's where I see the parallel to social media, and more specifically—Twitter.

Since Twitter is word of mouth on steroids, and the people who you follow, or who follow you are from such a wide spectrum of humanity, you're tapping into a pool of people who are engaged, willing to help, and readily able to activate action.

If CNN Tweets to (it's over three million followers) a difficult question about government, odds are they'll get some pretty phenomenal answers. Why? Because CNN generates interest in this area, and has followers from all walks of life around the globe: Technology, politics, entertainment, finance, media, etc. Some of the greatest minds on Twitter are following @CNN.

So test my theory out. Ask your followers a question you think will stump them, and see what bubbles up. Let me know what happens, and send me a Tweet about it! @cdessi.

12 BLOGGING

"Don't focus on having a great blog. Focus on producing a blog that's great for your readers."

—Brian Clark

Blogging is easier than you think. Today more than any other time in history, there is technology available at your finger — tips that are totally free. Most technology is highly intuitive, and it should be easy to use if you have some exposure to simple programs like Microsoft Word. Personally, I love using WordPress. The format is very similar to creating word documents. The icons are easy to interpret, and the format is intuitive to understand optimizing for search engine optimization. After you write each post there are clearly defined areas where WordPress prompts you to add key words and descriptions of each post. You can easily upload and tag images, and add links. The format is simple, and if you've written anything on a Microsoft Word document, you'll have no trouble blogging. Put your name in your WordPress URL to help you be discovered easily. Purchase your URL on Register.com, or GoDaddy and redirect the URL to your WordPress blog. I hired a CSS coder (via Twitter) who helped ensure my blog looks professional. If you're not a coder, it's easy to hire one to help.

Take some time before you start to write and think about your passion. Write about what you know. No matter what the topic, I guarantee you have an opinion. As I've mentioned, I started my blog in 2007 on WordPress, simply because I was ambitious and felt I'd hit a glass ceiling of sorts. I wanted to share my expertise and ideas regarding affiliate marketing. I started very slowly and the more thought I channeled into the posts, the easier it became. I didn't realize just how many topics I'd an opinion on. I know this helped me land my next role as a vice president at Zanox. When I met with the hiring manager we discussed the opinions I'd expressed in three separate blog posts. He had been reading my content. The blog also added a new and unique way for me to get to know my new colleagues. They could review my posts to see that I knew what I was talking about. They also used the blog to get to know me personally because I didn't only write about affiliate marketing. I shared my personal life. At the time I was expecting my first child and I blogged about it often.

Approach your blog as if it were a journal. The more you open up, the more the content will resonate with readers, and the easier it will be to stand out from your peers. Consider your past work relationships. It's likely that the most solid ones didn't flourish because of work discussions, but rather by opening up and sharing something about your personal life.

Include links and images. These are essential in the early stages of blog writing. Nobody wants to read a blog devoid of images. Be clear, concise, and to the point with your blog title. Blogging isn't the same as article writing. You need to grab your audience in the title. An audience need to immediately understand what the post is about, and quickly decide if they're interested enough to read on. On Twitter, copying the title is essential. On Facebook, when you post to your wall, include a captivating image alongside appropriate content.

Your World is Exploding

Throughout your blog post, you should direct your reader to resources of trusted content providers. For **SEO** reasons make sure the link **URL** is appropriate to the word you're linking to. The more links you build and the more links that return to your blog, the better your **SEO**. There you'll come across the term **Page** Rank, which is named after Larry **Page** (co — founder of Google). Nobody knows for sure what the algorithm is to ensure a good **Page** **Rank**; but we know that the more links which point to your page, the better. The more you link to other sites via your blog, and the more traffic you generate for other sites, the more likely they'll be to link to your content. In a nutshell, links are essential to your success.

13 SUCCEED IN SOCIAL MEDIA

"Once the water is deep enough that you must swim to stay afloat, does it really matter how deep the pool is?"

—Seth Godin

This past summer I was asked by my friend Greg Kelly to speak at an event hosted on the Intrepid Sea, Air & Space Museum. Greg is currently the co-host of *Good Day New York*; previously was the co-host of *Fox and Friends* and a White House correspondent for Fox News. He is also currently a Lieutenant Colonel in the U.S. Marine Corps Reserves. He still works closely with the Marine Corps, and asked me to speak to them after we became friendly during my appearances discussing social media on *Good Day New York*. The event is an annual conference that the military holds to prepare their officers for the media landscape that they'll encounter during their careers. I was honored. I was also terrified. Greg gave me minimal detail about the event, only mentioning that Geraldo Rivera, Police Commissioner Raymond Kelly (Greg's Dad), Brian Wilson and Anderson Cooper had been speakers at the same event. Great.

The Intrepid is one of America's leading historic, cultural and educational institutions. It's also an aircraft carrier. The museum is centered on the carrier Intrepid (CVS-11), one of the most successful ships in US history. It's certainly one of the most unique attractions in New York City. I've been there as a tourist, but never to speak to a group of military officers. I couldn't for the life of me, figure out what I would talk about. I spent four days researching, preparing and reviewing the content of my lecture. I showed up early—really early. So early in fact that I was the only one there except the security guards (nice guys). I like to be prepared and early at these types of events. Greg seemed relieved to see that I had even showed up. Apparently he had spread himself thin, and hadn't been able to do the show that morning while he ran around the former battle ship ensuring his comrades were treated well, and assured to learn something from his lineup of speakers. I spoke for about 30 minutes, describing how social media has changed the trajectory of recent political history, and sharing what they should be aware of when engaging in social media. I was impressed by their attention, questions and engagement. I was held for about a half hour after the lecture discussing how social media had affected them each individually. The most dramatic moment (for me) came when a General who was in the audience approached me to discuss social media. I was fascinated, but not surprised to hear that if he shares certain information of his whereabouts he could potentially endanger his family. This was something that I had overlooked in my presentation and think is important to discuss here. Social media is not appropriate all the time. I shared the general's concern, and helped him to better understand that if he wanted to he could blog in a controlled and monitored platform. The blog would effectively open up lines of communication that may not have existed before, but still ensuring the safety of his family.

I was also amused to learn that one of the most intimidating marines in the audience (he looked like he was placed in the audience from central casting for a marine) approached me afterward and turned out to be one of the amiable guys ever. Colonel Michael A. LeSavage,

Commanding Officer in the 25th Marine Regiment has a daughter attending my alma mater Loyola University in Maryland. The Colonel seemed very encouraged (relieved almost) that I was speaking to him that day, ensuring that perhaps his daughter was getting the education he'd hoped for! After we connected that day I shared blog posts with the Colonel detailing the loss of the Captain of my Loyola Rugby team on September 11 — Sean Lugano. I told the Colonel he should share them with his daughter so she could share with her classmates the reason why their playing field was named *Sean Lugano Memorial Field.* Suffice to say that those posts were a powerful way for the Colonel and me to connect. He shared the post with his daughter as well.

When engaging in social media business (as in life), social interactions matter, whether you're greeting your boss first thing with a cheerful "Good morning!", or you're hugging a friend you've not seen for a while. If you put out love and respect, you'll get love and respect in return. Here are a few tips to help guide your business through social media. If you act like you do in everyday life, you'll be okay.

Be Social: Offer a platform where your customers can communicate with you. I'd recommend a Facebook page. When Mark Zuckerberg first changed the format of Facebook, everyone thought he was crazy for implementing a newsfeed such as Twitter. The man's a genius. Facebook is now perfectly suited for the viral spread of content offered by businesses, and it shows up in newsfeeds across the globe. If one company posts on another companies page, the content posted is there for all fans to view. This type of interaction ignites social sharing and social discovery of new content.

Be Co-Creative: Let go of the reins and stop being so fearful. Instead, choose to engage and be co—creative. If you have a fan page, talk to your fans. Ask them for feedback, poll them, and learn from them. They're the reason you're here!

Open Up: Like the old tag line for Lotto, "You've got to be in it to win it." Get started today by joining a social network, or starting a blog.

Be Rewarding: Now that you have fans and followers, let them know how much you appreciate them.

Offer contests and sweeps, and give them a reason to be there.

Be Evaluative: Conduct surveys, and read comments and ratings to help you improve your product. Customers are there because they want to be. The insight they provide is invaluable and it comes from a pure place. Following that feedback will guide you and your business.

During my phenomenal three days at the Web 2.0 conference in San Francisco, I had the opportunity to hear from Bob Buch the former vice president of business development at Digg Bob said something that stuck with me, and still resonates today: "Social media is the ultimate bullshit meter."

As I continue to grow Silverback Social I chose to build a company around the values that I hold true. I know that we'll service our clients to the best of our ability, we'll be honest, and we'll create a culture of truth.

Clients choose to work with us because they understand our work ethic, and they're drawn to like-minded people who want to help them reach their goals. When I reached out to a friend recently we spent 90 percent of our meeting discussing all the "vaporware" out there. Companies may have great technology, but they get in their own way when they promise clients the world. I've seen this time and again while I've worked in digital media.

The main reason why some executives are slow to use social media is because at times, there's an element of snake oil salesmanship that tends to go hand and hand with new developments in the online world.

We're in a Darwinian world, for sure. However social media has the tendency to speed up the identification of untruthful brands. Technologies are rapidly identified as sub-par. Brands miss out on customer service opportunities, while those that go the extra mile are touted as heroes.

So why do nice guys finish first in social media? Why are the brands that are doing it right, excelling so rapidly? People *trust them.*

If they don't trust them, they can access information about a brand, technology, or service in mere seconds. What used to take months of research can be gleaned in a quick review of blog comments, community chatter, and Twitter and Facebook newsfeeds. The crème rises to the top because brand advocates can communicate their delight. On the flip side, they can also shout about a failed order, poor customer service, or unmet goals.

Your World is Exploding

I have been astounded by the business that Silverback Social has generated by word of mouth. Our team delivered and delighted each of our clients. We don't need to advertise because our clients told stories to their counterparts. The pebble rolled down the mountain, fast turning into a raging snowball, then an avalanche of positive chatter. If we didn't deliver we would have been out of business in a flash.

In social media, the nice guy has the opportunity to finish first, excel, and soar beyond all the competition. The companies that instill this mentality into their culture will crush the competition. Think of this amazing customer service story from Zappos; an online shoe and clothing shop where employees are trained to go beyond filling orders. Tony Hsieh the CEO shared two anecdotes that exemplify how Zappos workers think:

A woman ordered a wallet, tried it, out and returned it. Unwittingly, she had left $150 in the wallet. For days she accused her young children of pilfering from mommy. Then she received a note from a Zappos warehouse clerk returning the lost bills. The clerk, who made only the minimum wage, could have kept the jackpot, Hsieh noted. Zappos also could have hired more warehouse security to prevent theft. But the CEO suggested that it's more cost effective to hire honest people in the first place.

Hsieh was asked why more companies don't adopt the Zappos business model. "Patience," he said.

Most corporations don't want to put in the time to build customer service and a company culture. "It's whether you're willing to make that commitment," he said. I don't know about you, but for me that story resonates. It goes way beyond just "good" customer service. Now this story is "out there" in a social ecosystem. I pulled it from the Knowledge blog by WP Carey School of Business, and now I'm sharing it with you. I'll Tweet this story, post it on Drive Action Digital's blog, and post it in our newsfeed on Facebook. Zappos are the nice guys, and they're winning.

14 GET TO WORK

"A dream doesn't become reality through magic; it takes sweat, determination and hard work."

—*Colin Powell*

For a brief time growing up, I had an obsession with two things, and two things only: sports cars and the New York Yankees. I had posters of Ferrari's, Porches, and Lamborghinis posted throughout my room. These cars shared wall space with my beloved Yankees: Don Mattingly, Willy Randolph, Ron Guidry, Ricky Henderson, and Dave Winfield. My allegiance eventually evolved to include the heavy metal thunder I described in Chapter 9, but as a young man it was only exotic cars and the New York Yankees. Mom and Dad would always encourage me to post photos of the cars. Telling me "save your pennies" and "work hard" and you'll have one someday. I believed them. They said the same about becoming a New York Yankee, but I digress. Truly, the lesson was invaluable. Somewhere, somehow along the way this sentiment devolved in our culture.

When you see a guy drive down the street in a Ferrari it should piss you off, but not because he has more than you. It should motivate you to work harder. It should prompt you to learn more, read more, and know more than the next guy. It should provoke you to originate your own destiny, and create something. Stop whining, and pointing fingers, and just get it done. There is no reason why anyone with the technology available for them today should ever have to complain about their job ever again. In the interim, while you're cultivating your personal brand, and while you're curating your content, put your head down and work you ass off.

Recently, after an on air interview, a female news anchor (filling in for the regular anchor), shook my hand and said "Chris, it all just seems like so much work" to which I replied "you have to do it, for your career." I know I didn't convince her. I also know that soon, someone with a better grasp of social media will take her job. She will no longer be called to fill in for the regular anchor, and she will effectively make herself an obsolete contributor in the media landscape. The team at Silverback Social find ourselves in the midst of a daunting uphill battle to help articulate to the non-believers why social media is essential for their personal brand, and for their future. We present a case study regarding how protests are accelerated by social media, and they don't believe it's powerful. We discuss revolutions that were started on Facebook, and they retort stating that real media moguls don't use social media.

My Father always says that life is 10% what happens, and 90% how you react to it. At first I would get frustrated, but I now see their cavalier attitudes as my advantage. You should too. Now you know how powerful social media is, and you have a fresh view on how information is exchanged in our society. Those who don't adopt these technologies will be left behind for dead. They fail to see that it's already changed. They are already obsolete.

You have the tools at your fingertips to amplify your hard work. Touch this proverbial third rail of power surging through the social media ecosystem and unleash your intellect, insight and soul on the world. Those captains of industry, who think they're in control sit in their corner offices and profligate their caviler attitudes regarding social media, let them. Allow those cynics to scoff at Twitter, and mock your blog posts. The pure beauty of it all is that because technology is moving so quickly these unsuspecting pessimistic doubters don't even realize that they're already no longer in power. You are. You control your own destiny. You can only control what you do, how you react, how hard you work, and how you handle the situations presented to you in your life. Get into the office earlier, and stay later. Magnify, elaborate, enlarge, and intensify every interaction you have with your network via social media and be heard. Be patient and allow all of your hard work to swell behind you, surge, and sweep you up in a tide of your own making. You no longer have to wait to be discovered, you no longer have to wait in line, and you no longer have to plot, and maneuver through the gatekeepers. Don't let this opportunity slip through your fingers. Embrace these changes and see that your world as you once knew it is exploding. Grasp the philosophy I have presented, and clutch to the tenants of truth and fulfillment. Give, let go, offer and release so that you may seize this colossal opportunity.

15 SOCIAL SUMMARIES

"We are CEOs of our own companies: Me Inc. To be in business today, our most important job is to be head marketer for the brand called you."

—*Tom Peters*

Job Seekers

Everything has changed, so evolve or die. When hiring managers review your resume the first thing they'll do is to Google your name. It's up to you to own those results. You must have a hand in each of the results that you see. Whether it is via your blog, your Twitter account, Facebook page, or Quora profile this is your chance to let your personality shine. Allow your intellect to jump off the page. Share the video of your speaking engagements; and create your own blog with daily musings on your industry. Offer quality content and differentiate from the herd. Own your own brand. Don't allow old content to tarnish that image. Continually create new and engaging content to ensure you're at the cutting edge of everything happening in your industry. Let go of control and allow your personality to shine through. The company that doesn't react isn't the one for you. The one that does react will be the best fit for you.

College Students

Start now. Don't wait for graduation day to get excited about finding a job. Begin blogging, Tweeting and generating content that interests you. You are at a distinct advantage. You have come of age with this technology at your fingertips. Understand its power and funnel its energy toward a career that will fulfill you. If you understand the spiritual side of social media, you'll also understand that you can effect social change by leveraging these free tools. Don't sit idly by. Jump in and start now. There is nothing stopping you. It's free, and you already know how it works. There are no excuses. Be fearless.

Who knows, if a job doesn't present itself, you may identify your passion and start a business! Use technology to pre-qualify your potential employer in advance. Just like they'll conduct a Google search on you — you have the ability to conduct your own due diligence on them. Learn as much as you can about your hiring manager and the executive team. Seek context. As you take your first step into the work pool this is the most important bit of information you can glean—context.

Businesses

Listen, engage and allow for the conversation to happen around your brand. Allow your happy customers to have a platform to share your product and ideas via social media. Don't fear feedback and dialogue. Social media will cost money and certainly demands sweat equity. If you don't have time to worry about social media, then you don't have time to care about your business. Convene, don't control. Perhaps you'll learn something about your business that will change it for the better.

Final Thoughts

People don't yearn to be liberated from their daily lives. They want to be more deeply embedded in them. I believe this is a basic human need. For the first time in history, this need can be met via technology. This can be era-defining. Social media is the first technological example of humans connecting on a deeper level, and it will only continue to evolve. I know this to be truth. I don't pretend to know anything other than what I have experienced. Now that you understand why social media is so powerful — embrace it and allow it to support our collective spiritual awakening. Social media allows for more human and interpersonal connections via technology, and for me, that's a spectacular revelation. I'm proud to call myself part of the social media revolution.

About the Author

Christopher Dessi is CEO of Silverback Social. He is an award winning digital thinker, television & radio commentator, blogger, and public speaker.

He is a contributor on Fox Business Varney & Co, and Good Day New York. He is often called upon to lecture to businesses, Universities and government entities on the subject of social media.

He holds a M.S. in Direct Marketing from New York University (NYU) and a B.A. in Psychology from Loyola University in Maryland. He studied abroad during his junior year in Leuven, Belgium at Katholieke Universiteit's Erasmus Program.

He lives in Chappaqua, NY with his wife Laura and daughters Talia & Olivia.

Christopher G. Dessi